PRAISE FOR DR. JODY G. RAY

"This powerful book speaks to my two greatest fears when despair has entered my door: that I am the only one who has ever faced this visitor and that it will never leave.

"Through the stories in Pivot, Dr. Jody G. Ray reminds me that I am not alone, and also that it is not necessary for me to have what it takes to move through my challenge, since God has what it takes. In his book, Jody shows us a practical plan of action to face despair, allowing us to pivot and move toward balance and healing.

"This book may have been written by a pastor, but it is as valuable for the unchurched as it is for those of us in the pews each Sunday. Jody assures us that we are all in the wondrous journey of life together, needing each other—not to see through us, but to see each other through...with God's powerful presence and love."

—CLAIRE BOWEN, PRESIDENT OF
CLAIRE BOWEN AND COMPANY

"Hope is packaged and sold in many different ways in our society, often wrapped with false promises and an unrealistic view of life. This is why Pivot is such an important book. Dr. Jody Ray deals openly and honestly with the disappointments and pain we experience, pointing us to a hope that endures, sustains, and overcomes."

—PETE WILSON, BEST-SELLING AUTHOR
OF *PLAN B* AND *LET HOPE IN*

"Dr. Jody Ray writes from his heart to yours about those key moments in life that determine your future. With warmth, insight, and raw personal honesty, he unpacks the problems we all face and equips you to walk through the challenges and seize the future that God desires for you."

—WES AND JOY GRIFFIN, INTERNATIONAL
LEADERSHIP INSTITUTE

PIVOT

PIVOT

EMBRACING THE MOMENTS
THAT CHANGE YOUR DESTINY

DR. JODY G. RAY

LIONCREST
PUBLISHING

PIVOT
Embracing the Moments That Change Your Destiny

ISBN   978-1-5445-1394-2 *Paperback*
       978-1-5445-1289-1 *Ebook*

I dedicate this book to the most important people in my life.
First, to my wonderful wife, Shelley Lenore Ray. You are faithful,
courageous, and always encouraging me forward. Thanks for
your love and dedication to our family. I also dedicate the book
to three of the most adventurous, smart, and gifted children:
Jennings, Carson, and Robert. Each of you inspire me daily!

CONTENTS

FOREWORD

DON'T MISS YOUR MOMENT

We all have our moments.

You don't have to be a senior to have a "senior moment."

You don't have to be a kid to have a "Tinker Bell moment," with that airy spray of magic fairy dust that makes all dreams seem of numinous nearness.

You don't have to be an actor to have a "hammy moment," the playful, awkward, mawkish moment that leaves you with a lifetime of spine shivers.

You don't have to like greeting cards to have a "Hallmark moment," a moment so packed with preciousness, bathed in nostalgia, and shimmering in Kinkade kitsch that it deserves a card.

All romances have their "Casablanca moments."

Those who spend their lives in airport lobbies or government waiting rooms can testify to the "unforgiving moment," the fecundity of empty time when those moments in life that don't seem to add up can add up to very much.

Novelists design entire narratives around a "rubber ducky moment," a horrific incident in the past that scars and shapes the whole story, but doesn't appear until late in the narrative.

Photographers wait for hours, days, weeks for the "ongoing moment," when the shutter's brief opening and instant click capture a never-ending story.

Followers of Jesus can often testify to their "Pauline moments," when life boils down to singular (more than a single) moments, and you know once and for all who you are.

We worship and serve a God of every moment—of every disappointment, predicament, and environment. A God who gives us what Dr. Jody Ray calls, in his moving theology of moments, "pivot moments." But first, we must be attentive enough to receive these "pivots."

One of the worst things you can say of any person or organization is that "they missed their moment." There can be no "pivot moment" in an inattentive moment. The stories of missed moments are legion. One example is that Easter Monday, 1515, when Johannes Oldecop arrived at Wittenberg to matriculate at the university and found his first course with Martin Luther as his teacher. "I enjoyed listening to Martin's lectures," was all he said about this experience in his diary. Two things jump out at the reader about this: (1) the student called his professor "Martin," his first name, an equalization that is seen as a dismissal in German culture; and (2) he "enjoyed" Luther's lectures. Excuse me? Most scholars agree that 1515 was the most important year of Luther's life. It was when he wrote his commentary on Paul's Epistle to the Romans. It was when he was formulating the thoughts that would start a revolution and totally change the world. Here was a student who heard all of that, and didn't see or even suspect the radical implications of Luther's leaning other than to "enjoy" them.

Then, there were the thousands of students who missed their moment to study with Martin Luther King Jr. in the only classroom course he ever taught in his life at Morehouse College in 1960–1961. Or those passersby who

missed their moment by being unmoved by and unin-
terested in the last live concert given by the Beatles on the
roof of their studio, a reunion and a valediction captured
poignantly by Ron Howard's documentary on the Beatles
phenomenon. Or what about the whole city of Baltimore,
which ignored the death and funeral of one of America's
greatest writers, Edgar Allan Poe (1809–1849)? Less than
a dozen people attended his Presbyterian churchyard
funeral in Baltimore on October 8, 1849.

It is not often that we get a mulligan on these missed
moments. Those who disregarded the Poe funeral got
to redo that missed moment twenty-six years later in 1875.
The Southern poet Paul Hamilton Hayne (1830–1886)
was so troubled by the neglected, sodden state of Poe's
grave that he raised $1,500 to give Poe a monument.
During the ceremony that accompanied Poe's reburial
in a more respectable plot (his mother-in-law's), tributes
from Tennyson, Swinburne, and Longfellow were read
out loud. Walt Whitman attended in person. It was like
a "grand triumphal pageant," an eyewitness said, rather
than a funeral redone.

Dr. Jody Ray shows us in his book how to recognize our
"pivot moments"; how to both prepare for them and amp
and ramp them up so these moments become momentum; and how to open ourselves to receive new gifts of
"pivot."

Don't miss your moment by missing this book. You will hear God speak these words in its pages: *This is your moment; this is your time. Commit to it. Nail it. Let it rip. Bring it home. Go to church.*

LEONARD SWEET

George Fox University (Distinguished Visiting Professor)
Drew University (E. Stanley Jones Emeritus Professor)
Tabor College (Visiting Distinguished Professor)
Evangelical Seminary (Charles Wesley Professor of Doctoral Studies)

INTRODUCTION

When life is going well, we don't give anything a second thought. We cruise through life and go about the business of the day. We only question ourselves and our purpose during times of crisis, and that's exactly what I found myself doing in the late nineties. In a moment, my whole life changed, and my course was forever altered.

Before my life changed, I was an up-and-coming financial advisor. I worked for a small private firm; I was successful and moving up the ladder. My financial success had afforded me the opportunity to diversify and take on other business ventures. Life was really good! But all that changed when my wife of a few short years spoke the words "I want a divorce."

The painful memory of my parent's divorce from a decade earlier was still fresh in my mind, and at that time I had vowed it would never happen to me. My world was turning upside down. I was doing well financially, and life was good, wasn't it? I had been working hard and getting ahead—everything in my life seemed to be moving in the right direction. The stock market was booming, the world was standing on the threshold of a new digital era, and I was in a position to capitalize on it.

I had never failed at anything before—my inflated pride and ego wouldn't allow it. Divorce represented failure, and it was unacceptable; this wasn't supposed to happen to me. But it did.

A DARK SEASON

How could everything be great in one moment, and then fall apart the next? How could I be confident in myself, my work, and my life, and then end up wondering what happened and how I got here? I spent the next year questioning myself, asking, "Who am I? What should I do with my life?" All the worldly things that used to be important to me—the things I once lived for—no longer mattered. Everything I had worked for in the past seemed insignificant now. I felt lost. Insert tears, worry, and a whole lot of anxiety—I was in a dark season.

It doesn't make sense, but during the dark seasons of life, we often find that the most difficult days can become pivotal times; they mark our lives and give us clarity about our future. If you've lived long enough, you may know what it means to struggle through deep loss, brokenness, and pain. Most all of us have been there at some point along life's journey, and even though our personal experiences are different, those moments offer us the greatest opportunity to change and grow.

The most important thing I learned from my experience is that the person who walked into the storm is not the same person who emerged on the other side. I fought and I struggled; I wrestled with myself, and with God, and I *changed*. I still have some battle wounds, but I wouldn't trade them for anything in the world. Those wounds are a constant reminder of how God used a difficult time to set a new course for my life. I couldn't see God's plan or purpose inside the crucible, but I understood its refining power on the other side.

The presence of Christ gives us the assurance and hope that He will use dark days to bless our lives—and He'll do it in ways that don't seem possible in the moment. We often don't see the blessing at the time, but we can trust that God will strengthen our faith, deepen our roots, and build a greatness within us that will stand when the storm winds of life blow against us.

PIVOT MOMENTS

When I was sixteen, I heard God's call to ministry while attending a Camp Meeting revival service where my dad was leading the singing. That night, after the pastor's message, I walked across the sawdust-covered floor to a rustic altar and prayed intently about what I believed God was calling me to do. However, I spent the next fifteen years of my life running as fast as I could in the opposite direction. I heard the calling again several times in my life after that first night, but after my divorce, I was certain I would never hear it again. However, it didn't go away—it got louder.

Fast-forward fifteen years, and I'm a divorced financial advisor. While I was attending a business meeting in the Bahamas, a thought overtook me: "I'm not supposed to do this anymore. It's time to change."

After one of the meetings, I went back to my room and knelt down beside the bed. I prayed, "Lord, I know this is not what I'm supposed to be doing with my life. It's time to change course. Please help me. Lead me in the right direction." That night I made the decision that I would no longer follow Jody's plan—I would follow God's plan. I returned home from the trip determined to make a change; it was time for a new direction and a new life.

I quit my job, and everyone thought I was crazy. I have

to admit I thought I was crazy, too. The opportunity with this company was incredible, and success was almost certain, but I didn't care about that anymore—God was about to do a new thing!

One morning during that time of transition, I read the story of Joseph in the book of Genesis. Joseph faced an unimaginable crisis: he was wrongfully accused of a crime, arrested, and spent years in jail. As I read that story, I felt the Lord speak to me again. He said, "This is not the end. It is only the beginning."

Once I believed that things could be different, I surrendered. I knew I had to make changes in my life before anything could happen, so I went all in. As I began shifting my thoughts away from my problems and looking toward the future, I could see the beginning of a new path for my life. I'm a firm believer that God wants to do things in our lives that we can't even imagine. I also believe I received direction because I was looking for it. In a moment of clarity, I made a pivot, and my life has never been the same!

FOLLOWING GOD'S LEAD

After I started walking the new path God set before me, I had many impactful moments. These not only affected me spiritually—they impacted my life's circumstances.

They led to events that were beyond mere coincidence. I believe these moments hold the same potential for all who choose to surrender their future to God.

To give you an example, something incredible happened when I was actively pursuing my new direction in life. In the summer of 2000, I started talking with a district superintendent in the United Methodist Church about becoming a part-time pastor of a local church (even though there's no such thing as a part-time pastor). I wanted to keep my day job, run a business, and serve in the church on the weekends, or when I was needed.

However, after a lot of thought and prayer, I had a change of heart in the spring of 2001; I decided I was ready to go all in. I immediately called the district superintendent to inform him that I was going to leave my company, and I was ready to pursue a full-time position. He told me I was too late; there were no longer any available positions, but I should start moving toward becoming a candidate for ordination. The first step was to meet with a local board of pastors and laypeople from the area.

I was confident I was following God's lead, so he scheduled me to go before the committee. There were a number of candidates, and I was the last person to be interviewed that evening. As the interview progressed, one of the pastors asked me a series of unique questions, broader than the ones I'd been asked to prepare for.

When the meeting was over, the man introduced himself as the senior pastor of the United Methodist Church in Dahlonega, Georgia. He told me the church had an associate/youth pastor position available that they hadn't advertised yet. It was scheduled to start in one month, and he wanted to know if I was interested in the job. Of course I accepted the position. God had answered my prayer!

In a moment, God opened a door—one that would ultimately change the trajectory of my life. It propelled me on a magnificent, new course. I met my wife on this journey, and we now have three wonderful children. I entered ministry full-time and attended seminary. I met some of the most wonderful people who have become lifelong friends. I traveled the world and preached in some of the most incredible places. Ultimately, this open door led me to where I am today. I don't believe any of these events would have happened had I not followed God's lead.

A NEW DIRECTION

Crisis brings clarity, and I believe pivot moments are embedded within them. Pivot moments happen when we change course and go in a new direction. My desire is to help others see opportunities in the midst of difficulties—to define their pivot moments. I'm passionate about helping people find and embrace them. When we do this, these moments give us new direction, and they can change our lives. No matter where you find yourself today, and no matter how difficult life may be right now, you must believe that God has a greater plan for you.

I write this book not as a pastor or counselor, but as a coach. Without making light of the pain, I coach others to move through their emotions and circumstances so they will have hope for the future. I help them think from a new perspective so they can move forward. My goal is to help them recognize their pivot moments and give them the tools they need to make changes. I've been called to help people work through their crises, help them learn about themselves, and most importantly, help them learn who they are in Christ. One of my favorite Scripture passages in the Bible is 2 Corinthians 5:17 (ESV):

"Therefore, if anyone is in Christ, he is a new creation. The old has passed away; behold, the new has come."

When you understand who you are in Christ, you begin to see the world differently and understand that God has a purpose for you. Life is always more meaningful and joy-filled when we understand who we were created to be.

THE NEXT SEASON

Chances are, if you are reading this, you are walking through a difficult season of life. In the chapters that follow, I will share my own experiences, as well as stories about people who overcame times of crisis. All of them emerged from their difficulties understanding more about themselves and seeing God's greater purpose for their lives.

In this book, I'll help you gain clarity and embrace your pivot moments, and I'll share steps you can take to begin changing your situation from the inside out. All seasons have a beginning and an end, and we need to remember that a crisis is a season. Therefore, just as it had a beginning, it will also have an end. When we're in the middle of a crisis, it feels as if it will last forever, but it won't.

As you read, please keep this important statement in mind: how and when you advance into the next season of life depends on how you deal with the present one. The next season can be glorious and hold possibilities you've never imagined, so let's begin to move forward. You have a hope and a future. God is not finished with you yet!

CHAPTER ONE

EVERYONE EXPERIENCES A "MOMENT"

We do not remember days, we remember moments.

—CESARE PAVESE

Not everyone experiences the death of a loved one, a divorce, job loss, or another life-altering event, but everyone has a moment. We all have dark seasons of life. Part of being human is experiencing the full spectrum of thoughts and emotions. When we encounter the difficult, painful ones, we can't keep asking, "Why me?" We can't play the blame game, wanting others to bear the weight of our problems or take responsibility for them.

Most of us don't set out with the intention of wrecking our lives. We don't plan on encountering difficulties or walking down a wrong path, but certain situations change our circumstances. Oftentimes, these changes occur unexpectedly. My divorce wasn't planned. I woke up one day, my life was different, and I had to respond accordingly. I had to live through the difficulty. Similarly, many of our crises and dark moments are outside our control. We can't dodge them, run from them, or pretend they don't exist.

How we respond in a dark moment determines our direction. We can't give up and think, "My life is terrible. I don't have a future. I've made too many mistakes." We can't throw ourselves away. If we reach out to God in those moments, He will respond to us.

DAVID'S PSALMS

David, a prominent figure in the Bible, was a shepherd boy with no significant lineage. He didn't appear to have a bright future, and surely, he would never be chosen to be a king. However, David was called by God to do great things. From childhood to adulthood, his life was filled with events that prepared him for his future.

David was destined for greatness, but he made mistakes—huge, irrevocable mistakes—and some had fatal consequences. But God didn't give up on David or toss him aside. He didn't move on and choose someone else because he thought David was too far gone or no good. In the midst of David's messed-up life, full of adultery, murder, and brokenness, God was still faithful to David. He still used him. Even after all his mistakes, God said David was "a man after His own heart."

David also had struggles in his life that were not a result of his own choices. David had faithfully served a man named Saul, but Saul turned against David and wanted him dead. Saul relentlessly pursued David to the point that he had to spend time in hiding. He lost his home and community and had to live in caves.

David experienced life—what it means to be human. When plagued with situational depression and anxiety, he poured his heart out to God by writing psalms. He asked why this was happening to him—why were these his circumstances? He tried to do the right thing by serving Saul, but he found himself in a dark place and didn't know where to go or what to do. Here are several verses from the book of Psalms that clearly express David's anguish:

Psalm 18:6 (NIV)
"In my distress I called to the Lord; I cried to my God for help."

Psalm 69:1-2 (NIV)

"Save me, O God, for the waters have come up to my neck. I sink in the miry depths where there is no foothold. I have come into the deep waters; the floods engulf me."

Psalm 86:1-3 (NCV)

"Lord, listen to me and answer me. I am poor and helpless. Protect me, because I worship you. My God, save me, your servant who trusts in you. Lord, have mercy on me, because I have called to you all day."

David openly expressed his pain in his writing, but he also turned to God and praised him within his psalms:

Psalm 43:5 (NLT)

"Why am I discouraged? Why is my heart so sad? I will put my hope in God! I will praise him again—my Savior and my God!"

Psalm 46:1 (NIV)

"God is our refuge and strength, an ever-present help in trouble."

David's situation began to change when he cried out to God. The Lord promises to be faithful. He will never leave us or forsake us. Even when our love for Him fails, His love for us remains the same. He is always present and ready for us to come to Him. There is power when we turn to God, and He meets us in those moments.

CRISIS MOMENT EMOTIONS
ANXIETY AND FEAR

When we first enter into a life crisis, we can't see beyond it, and we often think it's going to last forever. We wonder what we are going to do, because there seems to be no way out of the situation. We think we are stuck, and we begin to feel anxiety and fear about the future.

Over time, anxiety and fear begin to control us: they evolve into worry, which is chronic. Worry creates an unhealthy thought pattern I call "circular thinking." We go around and around, fearful about the same thing over and over, expanding the scenario in our minds.

For example, if you lose your job, you might think, "I'm not going to get a job. I can't find a job. I won't have any money. I'm going to lose my house and my car. What if I get a job after I've lost my car? How will I get to work then?" This spiral of negative thoughts played out similarly for me when I got divorced: "I'll never get married again. I'm damaged goods. I'll never have kids."

Circular thinking is a waste of time and energy. We exaggerate the negative; we think much too far ahead and create a future in our minds that most likely will not happen.

You have to stop circular thinking in its tracks: don't give in, and don't give up. If you find yourself in this thought pattern, say, "Stop. This isn't going to happen. I'm not jumping to these conclusions."

SITUATIONAL DEPRESSION

Situational depression is a form of depression that occurs because of a crisis in our lives. When we experience stressful situations, we often react with symptoms of sadness, fear, anxiety, or even hopelessness. Situational depression often occurs when we have problems adapting to a new situation. For example, a job loss, divorce, or loss of a loved one can trigger situational depression. It's important not to ignore these feelings, because situational depression could develop into major depression.

LONELINESS

A recent Cigna study of twenty thousand US adults reports that almost five out of every ten people suffer from feelings of loneliness. Loneliness is a state of mind that causes a person to feel empty and alone. People who are lonely desire human contact, but their state of mind makes it difficult for them to make connections. Loneliness is not necessarily about being alone—it's about *feeling* alone. It doesn't matter if a person is by themselves or in a room full of people; they can still feel lonely.

Loneliness is a complex emotion because it is unique to each individual. For example, a lonely teenager who struggles with making friends at school will have different needs than a person who is recently divorced or one who has lost their spouse of many years.

If left unchecked, anxiety, fear, depression, and loneliness can impact our outlook on life and the choices we make. Some of the decisions we make under the influence of these powerful emotions can have difficult consequences. We may end up feeling worse than we did before, or we can negatively affect those around us. A friend of mine—let's call him John—experienced the consequences of this cycle.

JOHN'S STORY

John came from a great family, and he was a handsome guy. He also had great athletic abilities. His good looks and athleticism made him very popular in high school and in his fraternity in college. John lived in a world full of opportunity, and he appeared to have everything going for him. However, in college, he made some unfortunate mistakes. The fraternity and party scene were too much for him, and he began to drink heavily. At first, it was only on the weekends, but it became an everyday occurrence. His heavy drinking led to drug use that became an addiction. He eventually lost his scholarships and was forced to leave school.

John began to spiral downward. He thought, "I've completely screwed up my life. I've lost my scholarships. I have no future. I can never get back to who I once was." The spiral of negative thoughts led him into depression, and he isolated himself from others.

John's parents tried to help him, but John didn't respond well. He continued to lie, manipulate, and even steal from them. He was no longer connected with his friends from school, and he even found himself living on the streets for a time. He felt as if nobody would listen to him or understand his situation—nobody could help him. He continued to medicate himself to numb the pain. Since John felt like a failure and didn't think there was a way out of the situation he had created, he continued further down the dark path of addiction.

You might think John's downward spiral was natural. He made choices and was living with the consequences. But it doesn't matter whether we're hurting because of a choice we've made or an external circumstance outside of our control; the emotions of the downward spiral are similar.

SUSAN'S STORY

Susan was forty years old when her healthy and athletic forty-one-year-old husband was diagnosed with cancer. He passed away six months later. Susan was beautiful inside and out. She had much to enjoy in life, but she couldn't get over her husband's death. All she could think and talk about was his death. She was stuck in the pain of that moment and couldn't move past it.

Susan loved her husband and was fully devoted to him; her pain was overwhelming. The life she pictured for herself and her family disappeared when he died. Five years later, she still hadn't accepted her circumstances.

Both John and Susan were in the midst of darkness and couldn't see the light: they were stuck. They needed help to move through their season of crisis and to see the greater future God had for them.

MOVING BEYOND THE MOMENT

A crisis can be overwhelming. It can overtake you. When we are hurting, we want the pain to go away, and we'll do whatever we can to make that happen as quickly as possible. Instead of waiting for God, listening to Him, and pursuing Him, we seek other solutions. We might rebound into a new relationship or medicate the problem, but those are only temporary fixes. They don't heal the pain. By working on ourselves and allowing God to work in us, we can move out of our situation. We can come out of a dark season and move into a new one.

If we want to maneuver through a difficult moment, we need to define where we are. You'd think that would be easy: just define the crisis. But many of us don't even get that far. We continue to make excuses, keep asking why this is happening to us, or think that God is "punishing" us. If you are still thinking these thoughts, you've yet to define the moment.

Our circumstances are never as good as we think they are, but they aren't as bad as we think they are, either. Your life isn't over, and when you find yourself falling into circular thinking, you must recognize it and put a stop to it. Once you've reached this point, you will be able to assess the reality of your situation and see your circumstance from a different perspective.

If I were your coach, I'd listen to you and try to understand your story. Then, I'd help you define where you are. Without minimizing the pain or pushing it aside, we'd identify the starting point as "ground zero," and then we'd discuss where you'd like to be. I'd ask you to paint and describe an ideal picture of your life—what you want it to look like. What are your goals and dreams?

Then, starting with where we are at the present moment, we'd set goals and chart a course for achieving them. We wouldn't strive for perfection; we'd simply create a plan to move forward and get closer to the picture you described. You might already know the steps you'd need to take, and it's just a matter of getting started. Or it's possible you won't know what the second step is until after you take the first one. The important thing is that you take the step and make progress toward finding your purpose.

Finding someone who can help you embrace your present reality and, by faith, move into your future is an important part of moving forward. You could seek out a counselor, a pastor, a trusted friend, or a family member—anyone who can help you move forward. Choose someone who would be a helpful, positive influence and can keep you accountable to the process. Just know you have to do the heavy lifting. It's up to you to move forward.

Remember this: a mistake is an event, not a person. You aren't defined by your circumstances, and the crisis is not the end. The crisis is the beginning of something wonderful and new if you put your faith in God, trust Him, and believe He can and will meet you in your moment.

He can turn your life around. You can begin this process of healing with a person you trust, but you must work through it for yourself, with God's help.

FAITH IN ACTION

So, what does it look like to recognize our crisis moment, move beyond our pain, and seize our God-given future?

JOHN'S OUTCOME

John had been in and out of several rehab programs. He wasn't complying with them and kept getting kicked out. Eventually, he realized he had to commit to a rehab program if he was going to get better. He wouldn't be able to move forward if he was stuck in the cycle of drug and alcohol addiction, and he needed outside help to overcome it.

John didn't come to this realization instantly—there were setbacks. He and I began spending time together. We read Scripture and talked about life, and I could see he was slowly releasing himself from the prison of his crisis.

To make progress from that point, John had to create a plan. His next steps were finding a job and a place to live. Then, he wanted to go back to college. He had lost his scholarships when he was a freshman, so he had to start over from the beginning.

John completed the first two steps of his plan. When he returned to school, he began dating the girl who would later become his wife. John took the initiative to leave the past behind and move on with his life, but he couldn't do it alone. He placed his faith in God, and God helped him move beyond the crisis.

If you saw John today, you would never know he had a rough past. He is married with two children, and he is a respected businessman in his community. He is on fire for Christ and doesn't hesitate to share the story of what God has done in his life. John recognized he had much to live for. He saw that God wasn't finished with him yet.

SUSAN'S OUTCOME

Susan and I met, and we defined where she was. She had spent the last five years of her life reliving her husband's death over and over. She hadn't made any progress toward healing. All this time, she thought she was honoring her husband by mourning him, but she finally saw the light. Loneliness and dwelling on the past were not only affecting her, but they were also affecting her son.

Susan had to surrender and embrace what had happened to her. It was unfair and it certainly wasn't her choice, but it was her reality. She knew she needed to move forward, not only for herself, but also for her child. She said she wanted to move forward in life, fall in love and have a family, and have a father for her son.

After she expressed her desires and decided where she wanted to be, it was time to take the next step. It was fine for her to meet with me initially, but in order to truly open up and move past the pain, she needed professional help. Her next step was seeking out a counselor who could help her process her grief.

Susan recognized she had an opportunity to begin a new life. It was a pivot moment. Once she believed she had a future, things began to change. It took some time, but today Susan's life is a wonderful example of God's ability to transform. She went on to marry again, and she and her husband have added children to their family. The healing that has taken place for her is beautiful.

NOT AN ACCIDENT

During hard times, we may feel as if we've done something wrong; we've done something to "deserve" our difficulties. I don't believe God causes bad things to happen to us. I don't believe I was predestined to get a divorce and Susan's husband was predestined to die at a young age. I don't believe God causes our crisis moments, but I do believe God can use them for our good and His glory. I believe God can take those difficult moments in our lives and use them to help us see Him more clearly and understand His purpose for our lives.

I've learned there is a deep relationship with God that can only be experienced in the midst of a dark season in life. It's difficult to understand and even more difficult to describe, but there is a deeper level of intimacy with God that we can only experience when we walk with Him through times of crisis. Even though I shudder when I think back on all the pain I experienced over the span of ten years—and I would never return to those days—I wouldn't trade them for anything else in the world. Without the pain, I wouldn't be where I am today. I leaned on my faith in Jesus during the hard times, and by doing so, He led me to my destiny. I truly believe God will do this for all of us, if we let Him.

My prayer for you is that you will put your faith in God, no matter the circumstances or crisis you may be facing right now. You will begin to look for and find the opportunities that exist in your pivot moment. You will embrace your failures, your situation, and your heartache. When presented with opportunities, you will seize them, and you'll move forward into the purpose I believe God has for you.

CHAPTER TWO

EMBRACING YOUR MOMENT

Life is a succession of moments. To live each one is to succeed.
—SISTER MARY CORITA KENT

We all face painful, difficult, even gut-wrenching situations in life. The length of these moments is often determined by how we respond to them. When we choose to move forward in faith and ask the people around us for help, this creates pivot moments.

Difficult moments seem to linger on forever, and bright moments end too soon. Whatever the moment, it's not a brief flash in our life's history. It's a season, and how we enter a season determines its length and our success in it.

You have the ability to influence the outcomes of the difficult seasons you experience by how you walk through them. In Psalm 23, David says, "Even though I walk through the valley of the shadow of death, I will fear no evil, for you are with me" (ESV). David was in a dark valley, but he didn't consider staying there a possibility—he was going to walk through it. Notice he also said he wasn't afraid. He knew God was with him.

We need to approach all of our moments—the good, the bad, and the ugly—the same way David did. Enter each moment knowing (1) you will walk through it, and (2) you don't need to be afraid, because God is with you.

If you enter the valley and stop walking, that's where you'll remain. However, if you keep moving, you will reach the other side. Entering a difficult season in faith, and in a positive and hopeful way, will help you move through that season successfully.

A CHURCH CHALLENGE

Some years ago, I was appointed to a new congregation in the Metro Atlanta area. It was a predominately white congregation located in a community that was experiencing rapid demographic change. That transition, along with a slowdown in the economy, caused the church to experience a decline in attendance and weekly offerings.

This put the congregation in a very difficult position. It forced them to make drastic cuts in the church's budget to meet their monthly obligations, including paying their mortgage. They were in a desperate situation.

All of those circumstances justified my entering the moment with a negative attitude. I admit, initially, I didn't handle the situation in a positive manner. I struggled at times, kicking and screaming, saying, "Lord, why do I have to deal with this? Why do I have to be here?" Keeping that outlook would have been disastrous.

I finally came to grips with the notion that God had called me to this moment—my appointment to this church was an opportunity. There was something for me to learn and do here. I realized that an important part of moving through this moment was to embrace it—to start looking for inherent opportunities instead of focusing on the endless circle of problems.

Serving that church became one of the most meaningful times of ministry I've ever experienced. The leadership of the congregation came together as a group and began praying. We discussed a new direction for the church. What had God called us to do? Who was God calling us to be as a church? What ministry need could our church meet in the community? We began focusing on the future and moving forward in faith. Our focus turned to finding solutions to our financial situation and reaching the community, rather than keeping our eyes fixed on the problems. Over the next few years, the church was transformed.

The church became an integral part of the community. It became known as "the church that loves kids." Through a dynamite recreation program, a backpack ministry in the local elementary school, and a ministry to the high school football team, the church began to grow. Over time, it began to look more and more like the community around it.

The church also began to move beyond its financial struggles. Through prayer and moving forward in faith, again, doors began to open. Through a friend of the church, a very prestigious law firm in Atlanta helped us navigate our financial struggles. He guided us through the process and helped us negotiate with the local bank. There was no way the church could afford his services, but he and his firm worked with us and orchestrated a blessing.

The church's mortgage payment was reduced to less than half the original amount. The debt was also reduced, and new terms were set to help the church get back on track to financial stability. But the greatest moment came when I received the attorney's bill for his services, just before Christmas. When I opened the bill, it listed the hourly fee and a total at the bottom, but the "amount due" line only had one number listed: zero. At the bottom, the attorney wrote a note that simply said, "Merry Christmas!"

When we embrace the difficult moments in our lives— looking for the opportunities that exist—it creates momentum that propels us forward. Looking back on that season of ministry, I believe the power was in how we entered the moment. We saw God in the midst of the uncertainty; He was present in what appeared to be an impossible situation. There were challenges, uncertainties, and the possibility of complete failure, but we entered that moment with a positive outlook. Searching for opportunities opened doors we didn't even know existed.

When we're in a difficult situation, we tend to look at the past. We beat ourselves up, saying and thinking things like, "If only that could have been different," or, "If I had done this instead of that, I wouldn't be in this situation today." We need to let go of the past, embrace the present, and move forward, allowing God to do His work in us.

There are opportunities in every challenge we face. Whatever moment we're in, we need to embrace it, be fully present, and then look for those opportunities. When we do, God opens doors we don't even know are there. Thinking differently causes you to live differently, and positive momentum can make good things happen in the midst of bad circumstances.

GOD'S PREPARATION

The issues that church faced were beyond enormous. Dealing with either challenge—the demographic change or the economic slowdown—alone would have been a big task, but dealing with both issues at the same time was monumental. It reminded me of David's challenge facing Goliath. When most of us think of the story of David and Goliath, we think of Goliath as a great, big warrior who could have completely destroyed David in battle. Traditionally, this story is thought of as "the little guy defeating the big guy." It is, in essence, but there's a whole lot more to this story—victory only summarizes the ending.

When it came down to preparation, David was far superior to Goliath. David approached Saul and said, "Hey, I believe I can defeat this giant." Saul immediately outfitted David with armor—a long, imposing sword, a heavy shield, and the other garments of a warrior. Saul said, "You're set, David. Now go out there and fight!" But David could not use the weapons or wear the armor.

David told Saul, "I can't wear this. I haven't proven them yet." In other words, David had never used the armor or weapons, and he was not proficient or comfortable with them. What did David do? He laid down the sword, removed the armor, and confronted Goliath with the weapons God had given him—the sling and the stone—the ones he knew how to use. He remembered the days when the bear and lion pursued him, and he defeated both with the tools he had. When he was shepherd to a flock of sheep and had to kill those wild animals in defense, he was preparing to face Goliath.

David's picking up the stones and approaching Goliath was equivalent to his taking a gun to a knife fight. The scenario is quite incredible when you think about it—a trained, proficient person armed with a sling and a stone could hit a target from three hundred yards away with incredible accuracy. The force of David's sling was a death blow from the beginning. Goliath was doomed the moment he stepped out to fight; the little guy won because he was ready. When we look at our problems and challenges through that lens, they don't stand a chance. We need to remember that God has prepared us to be exactly where we are right now.

GOD AT THE CENTER

We often put ourselves at the center of the story—it's all about how *I* feel, what *I'm* going through, how dire things are in *my* life. But what we need to do, especially when we are facing monumental challenges, is bring God into the center of the story. David made his share of mistakes, but he never failed to put God at the center. Before facing Goliath, David knew he could fight him, but not because he had the proper tools and techniques. He entered the battle because he knew God was at the center of the story.

Saul and his army were focused on how big and strong Goliath was—they saw themselves facing Goliath and the Philistine army. They didn't understand that the battle belonged to God. David was different. He knew it wasn't his battle—it was God's battle. David didn't trust in himself or his abilities, but in the power of God, and by doing so he proclaimed victory in advance. This was the mindset David embraced when entering the ring. David simply said, "The Lord who rescued me from the paw of the lion and the paw of the bear will rescue me from the hand of this Philistine" (1 Samuel 17:37 NIV).

When we face situations with our families, children, careers, and any other area of life, it's our natural instinct and habit to put ourselves first. After all, we are human. We throw our problems and pain to the center of the story, because the feelings are real and raw. However, when we begin to see God at the center and realize He is with us, wonderful things can happen.

With God at the center, we can place our faith in His plans for us. We can say, "God, something happened;

something was done to me that was meant for evil, and I know you will make it better. I know you will make good out of the evil. You can turn the situation that tried to overtake and destroy me into something wonderful—I just can't see it yet. I don't understand all that is going on right now, but I believe you will see me through it, and there is something great on the other side."

I've had my share of adversity. My parents' divorce brought heartache, confusion, and anger. Shortly after the divorce, when I was a sophomore in college, my mother died after a long fight with cancer. I don't want to relive those experiences. They were painful, but in every one of those circumstances, I saw God at work. I believe what Paul says in Romans 8:28 to be true: "And we know that God causes everything to work together for the good of those who love God and are called according to His purpose for them" (NLT).

EVIL AND SUFFERING IN THE WORLD

We've all asked the question, "Why do bad things happen to good people?" I've certainly asked that question at certain times during my life, and it's hard to wrap our minds around it. Philosophers and theologians have also struggled with this question through the ages. They call it "theodicy," or "the problem of evil in the world." How do we reconcile the evil and suffering in the world with an all-loving and all-powerful God?

The Bible is full of people who wrestled with why God allows evil and suffering to exist: David questioned God repeatedly. Job cried out to God for answers. Habakkuk asked God why He allowed suffering and injustice to exist. The prophet Jeremiah complained to God, saying "Why does the way of the wicked prosper?" (Jeremiah 12:1 NIV).

A BBC reporter once followed Mother Teresa around Calcutta. Mother Teresa was caring for the poorest of the poor in the area; many of them were children who were starving to death and lacked proper medical care. The reporter, who was an atheist, said, "I can't understand why you would believe in a God who would allow terrible poverty to exist in the world." Mother Teresa responded, "Don't you go blaming poverty on God. Terrible poverty exists in the world because God's children refuse to share."

We can understand to some degree why there is pain and suffering in the world. For example, we know the following to be true:

- **We are finite.** We are organic beings made of flesh and blood. We live with limitations, like the laws of nature, gravity, human life spans, and bodies that are susceptible to disease.

- **Natural evil exists.** This type of evil is inevitable because we live on planet Earth. We experience occasional natural disasters like hurricanes, tornadoes, earthquakes, and drought. Part of life on this planet is that we are susceptible to forces outside of our control.
- **Moral evil exists.** This evil occurs because of choices made by humans who exercise their free will. People can use their free will to do evil things, and this causes much pain and suffering. Some people choose to crash airplanes into buildings; others choose to bring guns to schools, concerts, or churches, with the intent of shooting innocent and defenseless people. It's heartbreaking, but unfortunately, there are people out there who make these choices.

God is love; He is not the author of the evil in this world. God doesn't make bad things happen, but God can use our worst moments to do great things in and through us. God is the Great Redeemer. God can take our pain and turn it into our gain. People can use their free will to cause pain in our lives, but God's grace can redeem and restore. When we have been abused, lied to, or experienced the pain of divorce or death, God can take those moments and create pivot moments to change the trajectory of our lives and propel us toward His greater plan.

Through our times of stretching, difficulty, and pain, God

is able to do something wonderful in us, and in our lives. I've come to realize there is a depth of relationship with God that only comes through pain. Again, I can't grasp why it works that way, but the pain I endured in the past has made my relationship with God richer and deeper. Many of the successes I experience today can be traced back to painful times. When we remove ourselves from the center and put God there instead, we can begin to see through eyes of faith—we begin to see what God is doing. A door will open: you'll have an encounter with someone, or a new relationship will develop; something extraordinary can happen in your life that you never could have planned. Place God at the center when you face Goliath. Remember, it's *His* battle. It's *His* power and strength working through you.

Had there not been a Goliath, there would not be a kingdom. David would not have worn a king's robe or king's crown, and Jerusalem would not have become the city of David. He would not be forever etched into the history of God's people. David weathered many storms—he had many difficult moments to embrace, but Goliath was the one who opened destiny's door. Face your Goliath. By placing God in the center of your situation, you can transform your moment into a pivotal one that takes you to the greater future God has for you.

ENTERING THE MOMENT

Momentum is defined as the strength or force gained by motion or by a series of events. How we choose to enter a moment determines whether it has positive or negative momentum. One of my favorite ways to explain this is Newton's Law of Inertia: a body in motion stays in motion, and a body at rest stays at rest. His model focuses on the physical, of course, but this law is true in a spiritual sense, as well.

How we face our Goliath moments determines how we will travel through seasons and face obstacles. When we are in the middle of a challenging, dark moment, and the valley seems dry and endless, we must stay in motion. How we enter those moments determines the success of our next season and our momentum, so we need to grab them, hold on, and look for the opportunities that lie within.

POSITIVE AND NEGATIVE MOMENTUM

Positive momentum is a powerful force. It propels us in the direction of our goals, and toward a brighter future. However, if we don't commit to moving forward, negative momentum will take over.

Negative momentum is also powerful, but it propels us in the wrong direction. Negative momentum takes circumstances from mediocre to bad, or from bad to worse. Negative momentum builds when we fill our lives with bitterness, resentment, unforgiveness, and a refusal to acknowledge and learn from our mistakes. Negative momentum thrives on apathy, indifference, and bad choices.

THE SNOWBALL EFFECT

The winter of 2018 was unusually cold in Atlanta. The weather brought on an increasing amount of snow in an area that usually doesn't get much of it. Since we don't get much snow, we are sorely unprepared when it comes, especially if the snowfall is significant.

The forecast on a particular day that winter had only called for one inch of accumulated snow. Nine inches later, we had one of the largest snowfalls on record in our community. My normally fifteen-minute commute home from the church took nearly an hour. By the time I picked up the kids and got home, there was already a substantial amount of snow on the ground.

My kids were super excited. The moment we got home, they put on their jackets, grabbed their gloves, and immediately went outside to play. My eldest daughter said, "Let's build a snowman!" She bent down and started gathering snow to make a snowball. She packed it together with her hands and then placed it with the rest of the snow in our yard.

Then, she began the process of rolling the snowball around in the snow-covered yard. It was small, and she rolled it around and around. At first it didn't seem to be getting any bigger, but then I noticed it starting to grow; it was gaining momentum. The more she rolled the ball in the snow, the bigger it got, until finally the snowball had a twenty-four-inch radius. It was quite impressive!

As I watched my daughter make the snowball, I came to realize that circumstances in our lives are just like it. Both positive and negative situations work in this way. They start out small, and then build into something much bigger—rapidly picking up momentum—moving us in a positive direction or sending us into a negative downward spiral.

Negative momentum reminds me of the snowball effect, and unfortunately, I've witnessed the downhill spiral of this effect many times. One bad decision leads to another, and then another—gaining momentum with each decision until their full magnitude comes crashing down around us. In my eighteen years of experience as a pastor, I've found that most people don't deal with their life crises the right way. Most of the strategies we use don't propel us forward. They push us backward, keeping us from embracing opportunities that can change the trajectory of our lives.

CREATING POSITIVE MOMENTUM

John Maxwell was right when he said, "Momentum solves 80 percent of your problems." It is better to have momentum working for you, rather than against you. We gain forward momentum in our crisis seasons when we...

1. Define where we are
2. Develop a plan to move forward
3. Take the steps necessary to execute the plan

Momentum is a forward-moving force that is hard to stop once it starts. It happens when we refuse to back up, back down, or quit. Pivot moments occur when we allow the momentum of our activity to be powered by our "moment" with God. When we do this, victory is sure and imminent!

CHAPTER THREE

CRISIS AND THE PIVOT MOMENT

Many of life's failures are people who did not realize how close they were to success when they gave up.

—THOMAS ALVA EDISON

Life is a strand of constantly moving moments, and we remember all of them—the uplifting ones, such as a wedding or the birth of a child, and the challenging ones, such as the loss of a job or a divorce. When we go through a crisis, it's important to realize that it could be a pivotal moment in our life.

Pivot moments occur when you recognize that there is more to a situation than what you can see. They happen when you choose to believe you have a future, despite what your present reality might be. They occur when you choose to forgive those who hurt or betrayed you, or anyone who took you for granted. They happen when you don't allow your fears to paralyze you, and you don't let worries weigh you down.

The pivot comes when you recognize that the moment you occupy right now holds an opportunity for change. You are able to pivot, just like one would move on a basketball court—you're going in one direction, and then you shift (or pivot) and move in another. These pivot moments can be positive or negative. It all depends on your outlook when you decide to change.

CHANNEL FEAR INTO VICTORY

What prevents us from seizing our moments? What holds us back? It's fear.

Fear is a paralyzing emotion—it can imprison you, and it establishes limits in your life. If you fear heights, you will stay low. If you fear the outside, you will stay inside. If you fear people, you will remain alone. If you fear failure, you will never try. If you fear the future, you will stay in your present state. Fear is a deep and powerful emotion that can lock us in place and leave us feeling helpless to move.

The story of David and Goliath is not just about God preparing David to become a victorious king. It's also a story about two different men: David and Saul. One is gripped by fear, the other held by faith.

Saul was the king of Israel and led his troops into battle against the Philistines; the children of Israel were on one side of a valley and the Philistines were on the other. The imposing champion, Goliath, emerged clad in armor, ready to fight! He taunted the opposition in all manner of threats and arrogance.

Scripture says Saul and the Israelites were "dismayed and terrified" (1 Samuel 7:11 NIV). But David remained stalwart and said, "Let no one lose heart on account of this Philistine; your servant will go and fight him" (1 Samuel 7:32 NIV). David went into battle remembering that the Lord had rescued him from the paw of the lion and the bear—he knew God would also rescue him from the hand of this Philistine.

Too often, we are like the Israelites, and we let fear determine our future. But fear does not come from God; 2 Timothy 1:7 says, "God gave us a spirit not of fear but of power and love and self-control" (ESV). Power, forgiveness, and peace come from God. If we're trying to move past our mistakes or we're worried about a decision we need to make, God gives us the ability—the self-control—to make the right choices so we can move confidently into the future.

Allowing circumstances to paralyze us is detrimental to progress; it can ruin our future. We need to face them head on and realize it's not about whether or not we have what it takes to get through—it's about knowing *God* has what it takes. Hebrews 13:5 holds the greatest promise of God: "I will never leave you nor forsake you" (ESV). That promise doesn't mean we will never have problems or difficulties. It means that when we face those difficulties, God will be with us. Our problems won't dictate our future if we put our faith in God.

GABY'S STORY

I know a courageous woman named Gaby, and her story illustrates the power of letting go of fear. As a young girl, Gaby was smart and outgoing, but she had a difficult home life. Her family environment was far from healthy. Her father was never around, and he showed no signs of caring for her well-being. She also had a strained relationship with her mother at an early age, and it continued throughout her teens. When Gaby was in elementary school, her parents often left her home alone. Through these tough circumstances, Gaby learned how to survive.

When Gaby was a teenager, she gave birth to a son. She loved him dearly, and she did all she could to provide for him. Since she was young, it was extremely difficult. She worked several jobs to try to make ends meet, but every time she took a step forward, she encountered circumstances that pushed her two steps backward. She was frustrated and lonely, and at one point she considered taking her own life. She knew she couldn't continue this pattern, and she reluctantly gave up custody of her son.

To numb the pain, Gaby began drinking heavily and taking drugs. Still unable to make ends meet and in need of funding for her growing drug habit, she started working as a stripper in local clubs. The money she made wasn't enough to fund her lifestyle, so one of her friends introduced her to a high-profile pimp. She began working for him out of an apartment.

Gaby saw five to ten customers per day, and generally had only enough time between visits to freshen up for the next client. This went on for a number of months. One day, she came to a place where she felt stuck, frightened, vulnerable, dirty, and ashamed. She realized she had lost control of her life, and something had to change.

A short time later, as Gaby walked through a neighborhood, she saw a building with a steeple and a cross on top. She walked toward that cross, and she came to a big yellow church. She was determined to go inside and make someone pity her. She planned to cry to them, and tell them how bad her situation was, and that she didn't think she would live much longer. However, when she entered the building, there was no one there to listen—everyone had gone home for the day.

Disappointed that she was unable to carry out her plan, Gaby decided to enter the sanctuary. She sat down in the second-to-last pew from the back and waited, hoping someone would show up. No one came, so she decided to pray. When she finished, she found a prayer card and pen in the seat pocket in front of her and began to write. It wasn't a prayer request; it was a goodbye letter. She wrote her phone number on the card, placed it on the altar, and walked back outside to the world she hated.

The following week, Gaby received a phone call from one of the pastors of the church. Her name was Kelly and she asked if she could take her to lunch. Gaby agreed. At lunch, Gaby poured her heart out. She talked about her childhood and her difficult family life. She talked about how she missed her son. She also said she didn't like church and didn't believe in God.

Then, on a Saturday night that December, Gaby was pulled over, cited for a DUI, and arrested. She threatened to take her own life, so the arresting officer didn't take her to jail—he took her to the emergency room. She had hit rock bottom.

When Gaby was released, she was met by families from

the big yellow church. They took her to dinner and bought her clothes, Christmas presents for her son, and groceries for her home. She was ashamed, but grateful. She continued her relationship with the church and experienced overwhelming love from them. Every time she walked through the doors, she felt her heart was being mended and her mind was being shaped. She came to realize they were her family—she finally felt like she belonged.

Through the church, Gaby was introduced to a place called Wellspring Living in Atlanta, Georgia (WellspringLiving.org). Their mission and mantra is "We help women dream again." Wellspring offers residential and community-based programs that help transform the lives of those who are at risk or who have been victims of sexual exploitation. Gaby spent two years at Wellspring Living, and they provided the space and resources she needed to get help and get back on her feet.

With help from this new and inspiring home, Gaby was able to fully embrace the situation she was in, turn her life around, and graduate from the program. Fast-forward to the present, and she has a great job, has custody of her eight-year-old son, and makes public appearances to share her story and advocate for human-trafficking victims. Gaby is a living example of what is possible when we make the choice to move forward.

ADVANCING IN FAITH

During my doctoral studies, my mentor leader was Dr. Leonard Sweet. He organized our class into a "cohort," and he called our gatherings "advances" instead of "retreats." I asked him why he did this, and he replied, "Because Christians don't retreat. They advance." It was a simple yet profound description for what expectations should be in our Christian faith.

Since God has our future in the palm of His hand, we will always advance. If we find ourselves backpedaling, choosing not to forgive others, focusing on the past, or even clinging too tightly to the present, we will end up in a state that is much like treading water—we remain stuck in the same spot. God is the one who gives us the ability to advance!

Looking back at the story of David, we see that he was successful in his battle with Goliath because of all he learned through his life experiences. He learned about the heart of God and His faithfulness through his long days of shepherding his father's sheep. His need to protect himself from lions and bears led him to become proficient with a sling and stone. Ultimately, the things he learned during that time led to his defeating Goliath. David's experiences gave him a confidence that no other man in Saul's army possessed, and he was able to seize his pivot moment.

David's story shows that faith allows us to see beyond trying circumstances. Making the choice to push fear aside and move forward leads us into the future God has planned for us. When we can't see the finish line, we must continue to put one foot in front of the other—taking steps of faith to break chains and tear down walls. We can accomplish and experience more than we ever imagined if we recognize our pivot moments and trust that God is at the center of each one.

A LIFE IN MOTION

Life has personality, and it's constantly in motion. It moves forward, and it moves fast, through a string of seasons and moments. In the midst of each moment, there is the opportunity to change. We always have the chance to do more, or do better. Pivot moments lead to soul searching, and we ask ourselves questions like, "Where am I supposed to be in life? Where am I heading? What is God calling me to do? What's my purpose?"

Opportunities lie before us in every season, but the difficult ones offer destiny-making moments. Opportunity becomes crystal clear when we're between a rock and a hard place. I believe the size and difficulty of the moment determines the greatness of the opportunity.

That doesn't mean that if you are suffering, you are destined to become the king of Israel, but it could mean that a major shift in the direction of your life is ahead. The difficult season in my life helped me to gain clarity and the ability to see a new direction. There was a time when I thought I'd be in the business world forever, but the dark season helped me see beyond material wealth. I had a great calling to be a pastor, and in a pivot moment, I embraced it. My friend John, who was suffering from addiction, realized he was destroying his physical body, missing opportunities, and hurting his loved ones. In a pivot moment, he turned to face a new direction and decided to pursue a new life for himself.

IDENTIFYING PIVOT MOMENTS

The Eastman Kodak Company was once the world's leader in cameras, and renowned for its innovation. If you took pictures a few decades ago, then chances are you were using a Kodak product. Up until 1976, Kodak had 90 percent of the American market share for cameras, film, equipment, and photography. The company was so popular, the phrase "a Kodak moment" was widely used to describe an unforgettable life moment captured in a photograph.

In the late 1990s, the world began moving away from paper film and moving toward digital imaging. Kodak invented the digital camera in the midseventies, but the company didn't develop the new technology. Instead, they chose to table it because it was a threat to their core products and services. Ironically, Kodak missed its moment! In 2013, Kodak was able to escape bankruptcy only by selling off its patents for $525 million.

Like Kodak, we can miss our moments when we focus on the past or on our present reality. This is especially true when we're in the middle of painful circumstances. It's natural for us to focus on the pain when we're struggling, and we don't recognize the moment for what it could be—we can't see the opportunity that exists to shape our future.

When I coach people who are in the midst of struggles, I ask, "What opportunities are here for you?" The first time they hear that, they look at me like I'm speaking a foreign language. They're in a world of hurt, and I'm asking about opportunities? How can there be opportunities when they're in pain? The truth is we have to shift our thinking and move past the pain; we have to begin focusing on the future. Viewing our circumstances through the lens of faith will determine where we go from there.

We must be fully present in the moment to see opportunities. Looking too far into the future, or focusing too much on the past, won't allow us to see them clearly. When confronted with our pain, we want to do whatever we can to eliminate it as quickly as possible. We choose the path of least resistance and the moment passes us by, or we end up making choices that are less than ideal and don't lead to healing.

The path of least resistance is ever present in nature and science. A river always flows around a mountain instead of through it. That same river will always flow downhill instead of uphill. Likewise, electrical currents always move through the easiest route. Human nature is no different, and we often choose the easiest path, neglecting the *best* path. The path of least resistance is the least unpleasant or least painful route to take, but the life you desire and the future you want can't be found by avoiding pain.

If you want to make positive change in your life, it doesn't come by way of the path of least resistance—the best route is often the most difficult one. For example, if you want to get in good physical shape, you will never get there by sitting on the couch. You have to turn off the TV, go to the gym, and work out. Or if you want to build or enrich a relationship, you must invest your time and energy. In both cases, the path of least resistance won't get you to where you want to be.

We all have Goliaths to face. We can run away from a problem, but it will continue to resurface until we decide to deal with it. Divorce is often the path of least resistance for many couples. They choose to end a strained relationship instead of working on the issues that caused the problems. Then, they are surprised when they enter a new relationship and discover that the old junk has followed them there.

THE STORY OF JOB

Job is a well-known character in the Bible. He lost his family, his home, and his livestock all in one day. His friends gathered around him, proclaiming that the loss was Job's fault; he must have committed some sin or done something to anger God, and he brought this on himself. In Job 2:9, his wife even says, "Are you still maintaining your integrity? Curse God and die!" (NIV). By this she meant, how can you continue to follow God after all we have suffered?

Despite the barrage of negative words and thoughts, Job eventually reached a point of clarity. He realized that tragedies happen in life, and he refused to lose his faith because of present circumstances. Scripture tells us Job's latter days were greater than the days of his past—everything was restored to him, and more. By holding on to his faith and keeping God at the center, Job moved forward and climbed higher than he ever had before.

I recently counseled a woman whose husband had died

after a long battle with cancer. Through the course of our conversations, she said it was time for her to focus her attention on God's "Plan B" for her life. "Plan A" was gone, and now she had to settle for "Plan B." She viewed Plan B as a lesser plan; she thought it was second best. However, that's not how God works. I believe God gives us another "Plan A." The next phase of our life can be greater than the first! I wouldn't be where I am today relationally, spiritually, and professionally if I had followed through with what I thought was "Plan A" for my life.

CHOOSE YOUR RESPONSE

Pivot moments arrive in many different forms. Crises will come and go in our lives, and we need to recognize the pivot moments that exist within each one. Sometimes the crisis we face is the result of our own decisions and other times it is beyond our control. No matter the reason, all crises hold opportunity; we shouldn't be afraid of the future or have a negative outlook.

A good friend of mine, Robert, was part owner of a growing construction company. He managed projects in the field and his partner worked in the office managing the company's finances. One day, he received a call from their banker. He learned that a number of the company's checks had bounced and the matter needed to be resolved quickly. That phone call led to Robert discovering that his partner had been mismanaging finances, and the business was on the verge of collapse.

Robert was in shock as he found himself facing the possibility of his business closing and of financial ruin. The next morning, as Robert did his devotional, he read a quote from C. S. Lewis: "Hardships often prepare ordinary people for an extraordinary destiny." Those words of encouragement inspired Robert. He rallied his team, and with help from his wife, they paid off the debts within a few months. His formerly struggling business is now twenty years old and still thriving!

When faced with pivot moments, we can choose to respond in fear or in faith. We can choose worry and anxiety, or we can choose to put those emotions aside and move forward. It's important to remember that we cannot recreate a pivot moment. We may get another chance at a different point in time, but once the moment is gone, it's gone. Our choices during pivot moments have a profound impact on us, and every time we miss an opportunity, we lose time. We only have one life, and we want to live it to the fullest.

Embrace your pivot moments and move forward into your destiny by faith.

CHAPTER FOUR

CRISIS BRINGS CLARITY

The greatest power that a person possesses is the power to choose.

—J. MARTIN KOHE

There are many influences in the world, and they can have a tremendous, visible impact on our lives. Some of these influences cause us to make bad choices, while others lead us to good ones. It's estimated that the average person makes as many as thirty-five thousand choices per day. That's a lot! Our lives are shaped by the decisions we make—where we end up in life is the culmination of our choices. Many of them have far-reaching consequences, both good and bad. We like to think we are making the best decisions all the time, but how do we know if we are?

Our judgment can be clouded by fleeting moments of

strong emotion and impulsivity, which leads to making bad choices. Other times, our brain uses systemic flaws to justify them. These systems, known as *cognitive biases*, may make us feel better about poor decisions, but they don't change the fact that we were wrong. Many people don't want to be responsible for their choices, and they don't want to admit that their decisions have real-life consequences. Try as they might, they can't escape them.

Let's return to David's story to illustrate the impact of our choices. Some years after David became king of Israel, he sent his men off to war, but David remained in Jerusalem. One evening, as David walked around on the roof of his palace, he noticed a woman, Bathsheba, bathing on a neighboring roof. Bathsheba was very beautiful, but she was married to Uriah, one of David's lead soldiers. Nevertheless, David desired her and he sent messengers to bring her to his palace. David and Bathsheba committed adultery, and it resulted in her becoming pregnant with a child.

David's poor decision led to a string of problems. He sent for Uriah to return to Jerusalem, hoping he would sleep with his wife and believe the child was theirs. When Uriah returned home, however, he refused to be with his wife, knowing his fellow soldiers were away fighting. Even when David presented Uriah with gifts and got him drunk in an attempt to entice him to go to his wife, he still refused—he chose to sleep on a mat among David's servants. Uriah said, "The ark and Israel and Judah are staying in tents, and my commander Joab and my lord's men are camped in the open country. How could I go to my house to eat and drink and make love to my wife? As surely as you live, I will not do such a thing!" (2 Samuel 11:11 NIV).

The next day, David sent Uriah back into battle carrying sealed orders that he was to be placed "in the forefront of the hottest battle" (2 Samuel 11:15 KJV). Sure enough, Uriah was killed, along with a number of other soldiers who fought in the same deadly assault. David sent word with Joab's messengers that it was collateral damage—just a part of war—and Joab should not be concerned, but David knew in his heart that he had committed murder.

The pregnant Bathsheba was now a widow. After the customary seven-day period of mourning, David moved her into the palace and married her. All of this took place before she showed signs of being pregnant. It appeared that David's plan to hide his sin was going to work, but the Bible tells us, "But the thing David had done displeased the Lord" (2 Samuel 11:27 NIV).

God sent the prophet Nathan to rebuke David. Nathan said to him, "There were two men in a certain town, one rich and the other poor. The rich man had a very large

number of sheep and cattle, but the poor man had nothing except one little ewe lamb he had bought. He raised
it, and it grew up with him and his children. It shared his
food, drank from his cup and even slept in his arms. It
was like a daughter to him.

"Now a traveler came to the rich man, but the rich man
refrained from taking one of his own sheep or cattle to
prepare a meal for the traveler who had come to him.
Instead, he took the ewe lamb that belonged to the poor
man and prepared it for the one who had come to him"
(2 Samuel 12:1–4 NIV).

David burned with anger and said to Nathan, "As surely
as the Lord lives, the man who did this must die! He must
pay for that lamb four times over, because he did such a
thing and had no pity" (2 Samuel 12:5–6 NIV).

Can you picture the drama and intensity in that throne
room? Nathan looked squarely in the king's eye, slowly
raised his hand to point his finger at the king, and said,
"You are the man!" (2 Samuel 12:7 NIV).

I'd like to tell you this story has a happy ending, but it
doesn't. As a harsh lesson in reaping and sowing, David
and Bathsheba's baby died one week after he was born.
David's decisions had devastating consequences and
caused him a great deal of pain.

STRUGGLES LEAD TO PIVOT MOMENTS

What happened to David is an extreme example of negative impact. We don't always face a consequence like the one he did, but there is usually some type of consequence to our actions. When we make mistakes, we must come to terms with them and embrace the moment. It doesn't matter whether we've made a bad financial decision or we're stuck in a pattern of addiction or adultery—we must come to a place where we recognize what we've done. We need to say, "Yes, I did this. I made a mistake." It's difficult to accept responsibility for our choices, but it is the vital first step if we are going to experience a pivot moment.

I have a good friend who is well known in his community. He has a beautiful family and a successful business, but he had a drinking problem that eventually developed into an addiction to alcohol. He managed it quite well for a long time—no one outside of his family knew there was a problem. However, after a number of years, it was out of control. One night, while driving home from an office party, he was pulled over. He failed the sobriety test and was given a DUI.

At first, he made all kinds of excuses for his drinking, assuring everyone that he didn't have a problem. "Sometimes I drink a bit too much, but it's no big deal. I can stop anytime I want to. I never drink and drive; this was a one-time error in judgment."

He thought he had everything under control, but he didn't. His drinking had caused strife in his home and other areas of his life, but he kept a shield of denial in front of him. Ultimately, the DUI led to his acknowledgment of the problem, and just in time, too. He was close to losing his family and his business—his wife wanted to move out and take the kids with her. That possibility, along with the DUI, hit him hard, and he knew he couldn't continue on his current path.

He embraced the issue and began looking for opportunities. He declared that he was finally "working on himself." He vowed to walk away from alcohol for good and entered a rehab program. He started focusing on his relationship with God, his wife, and his children, and he emerged from the situation better than he was before. His season of alcohol abuse was trying, and rehabilitation was uncomfortable, but the crisis propelled him to work on his marriage and become a better father. His life changed for the better because he recognized his mistakes and embraced his pivot moment.

This story has a wonderful ending, but not all of them end like this one. Many times, people reject their problems or mistakes, and that opens the door to making more bad decisions—they continue to hurt themselves and their loved ones. We must accept the reality of the choices we made, seize the opportunity for life change and growth, and pivot in a more positive direction.

FAITH IN THE MOMENT

My wife, Shelley, is a nurse-midwife, and she's very in tune with the joys and trials of childbirth. When she was pregnant with our first child, everything appeared to be going well. We had nothing but great reports from the doctor and the pregnancy was moving along as expected. Well into the pregnancy, Shelley unexpectedly had a miscarriage. This began one of the most difficult seasons of our lives.

I remember at one point we were so overcome with grief and depression that I didn't think we'd come out of it. I was concerned for my wife—the weight of the sadness she experienced was difficult to bear.

Shelley's family knew we were struggling and asked us to come over for a visit; the whole family was going to be there for dinner. On the way to Shelley's sister's house, I received a call from a pastor. I didn't know him personally, but his name was familiar.

He said, "I know you've recently experienced a loss. I had a dream about you two, and I have some things I'd like to tell you. Would you be willing to talk with me?" We agreed to return his call, and did so when we arrived at her sister's house.

The pastor wanted to talk with both of us at the same

time, so I picked up a phone in the house, and she picked up another. He told us about his dream and said some encouraging things about our situation. He told us that although this is a painful time, God has a greater plan for our lives and future. His insight was surreal and inspiring. He told Shelley that God had heard her prayer from several days before, and he even quoted some of the exact words she had spoken.

At the end of the conversation, the pastor said, "Shelley, I know you will be pregnant again in ninety days." I was shocked and upset—I couldn't believe that he would say such a thing! I could tell Shelley was listening intently to every word he spoke, but she was emotionally fragile and I didn't want her to get her hopes up only to be hurt again.

After we talked with the pastor, I noticed an immediate change in her attitude. It was as if the darkness that had surrounded us for several months had been lifted and she was back to her usual self. The next day, she hung a calendar on our refrigerator and drew a line through each day as it passed.

On the ninetieth day, she called me at work and said, "Hey, do you know what today is?" Of course I knew, but I was nonchalant about it. I acted as if it was no big deal because I didn't want her spirit to be broken again. "It's the ninetieth day...and I'm pregnant!" Today, we have a beautiful daughter, Jennings, named after her grandmother.

Shelley recognized her pivot moment and made the choice to believe the pastor's words—she had faith. She believed God could change our devastating circumstances and create something great in our lives. Her choice to believe transformed us spiritually, and all these years later we still see and feel the impact of the change.

Today, Shelley speaks courage and comfort into the lives of many women in the Metro Atlanta area—she is honored to care for them. She delivers hundreds of babies each year, and we receive Christmas cards from many of the parents. Our heartbreaking experience served to enhance Shelley's midwife training and knowledge, and she continues to excel in her work and purpose.

RISE FROM THE GROUND

In David and Bathsheba's story, we can surmise that they felt the devastation of losing a child. As the mother, Bathsheba had a greater struggle with painful emotions. When the child was ill, David fasted, cried out to God, and prayed their son would live; but when he learned his child had died, he stopped fasting.

David rose from the ground, washed his face, changed

his clothes, and went to the House of the Lord to worship. Then, he returned home and requested food. In 2 Samuel 12, we read that David's attendants asked him, "Why are you acting this way? While the child was alive, you fasted and wept, but now that the child is dead, you get up and eat!" David replied, "While the child was alive, I fasted and I wept. I thought, 'Who knows? The Lord may be gracious to me and let the child live.' But now that he is dead, why should I go on fasting? Can I bring him back again? I will go to him, but he will not return to me" (2 Samuel 12:21–23 NIV). Then he left to be with Bathsheba and comfort her.

David and Bathsheba went through a time of healing, forgiveness, and repentance. They endured a difficult moment, but they did not stay there—they didn't remain depressed or sad. In the end, they received forgiveness and moved on with their lives, with Bathsheba eventually giving birth to David's successor, Solomon.

No matter how painful the circumstances, we must keep moving forward. I'm not saying numb the pain, hide it, or pretend it doesn't exist—we have to embrace it. The story I told about my wife and myself illustrates what can happen when we embrace a pivot moment and choose to move forward in faith.

EXTERNAL CRISIS AND INTERNAL REFLECTION

On May 4, 1968, on a quiet summer afternoon, my grandfather, grandmother, aunt, and uncle drove home from a trip to the grocery store. They lived on a narrow dirt road in the rural community of Chester, in Choctaw County, Mississippi. The drive that afternoon would have a tragic impact on my family. Just a few miles from their destination, they were in a head-on collision with their close friends and neighbors, the Prewitt family.

My family suffered severe injuries and had to be transported to Baptist Hospital, which was three hours away in Jackson, but the greatest hurt that day was the loss of my grandmother. She was propelled through the front windshield and instantly killed upon impact.

It took a number of months, both physically and emotionally, for my family to get beyond the trauma of the accident. During this time, my family had a choice to make. They could allow anger and bitterness to consume their lives, or they could choose to forgive. My grandfather said it never crossed his mind to hold the accident against the Prewitt family—they were friends. It was an accident, and they would need to help each other heal from the pain. I can't even begin to imagine the implications of that decision on the lives and health of our family. Even though tears come to their eyes today when they talk about it, there is no grudge—there's only love.

One of the passengers in the other vehicle was an eleven-year-old girl named Cheryl. She was thrown through her front windshield. Her back was broken and her left leg was crushed. Her face was also badly scarred, and she required more than one hundred stitches. The doctors told her parents there was a very good chance that she would never walk again. She was in a body cast for four months—it extended from her chest to her toes on one side, and to her knee on the other side. When the cast was finally removed, her left leg—the one crushed in the accident—was a full two inches shorter than her right one. She eventually regained her health and the scars healed, but her greatest healing came several years later.

When Cheryl was a senior in high school, she stepped forward to receive prayer during a healing service in Jackson. She believed that God could heal her, and He did. That very night, her left leg grew two inches!

If the name Cheryl Prewitt seems familiar to you, it's because she effortlessly glided across a stage in Atlantic City in 1979 and received the Miss America crown. Even today, she is considered the most sought-after Miss America in the history of the pageant. There were times during her reign when pageant officials asked her to "tone down" her faith-filled message, but she politely refused.

God took a tragic situation that could have broken two families apart forever and used it to make them stronger. They embraced their pivot moments and moved forward, and it chartered a course for them to live and love together. I believe our families have been blessed because my grandfather didn't get bitter—he chose to get better. That tragedy also gave Cheryl a platform to share the grace and love of Christ and how God healed her with multitudes of people.

HOPE AND HEALING

When we experience tragic events in life, like the loss of a loved one, the pain can almost be unbearable. We often deal with a number of different emotional responses. This is part of the grieving process, and it's important to remember that everyone deals with pain in different ways. The grief we experience with the loss of a family member or close friend can affect us emotionally, spiritually, and physically. It's important to grieve, but we must recognize that there are both healthy and unhealthy ways to do so.

For example, unhealthy grieving includes denial, depression, and a number of addictive behaviors. Unhealthy grieving occurs when the sense of loss becomes intolerable, and instead of dealing with our pain we act out in unhealthy ways. On the other hand, there are a number of ways to process grief in healthy ways, such as acknowledging feelings, seeking a grief counselor or support group, venting anger and hurt (rather than holding it in), exercising, and engaging in healthy, positive activities.

When we're hurting, we need to acknowledge where we are and begin the process of healing. If we don't move in a positive direction, it only compounds the problem and dramatically affects our future. I believe God can heal the heart, but that doesn't mean we forget our pain—we never will. I still see and feel remnants of difficult personal and professional circumstances from my past, but God has helped me to move past the pain.

In every crisis, we search for hope. When Shelley and I felt the agony of losing a child, the encouraging words from the pastor gave us hope. His words helped Shelley come to terms with the loss, and it infused her with the faith she needed to move forward. We learned a great deal from that pivot moment, and it has created our testimony as a couple: God is love. It's not what God does; it's who He is.

Because God is love, He always gives us hope and shows His love in mysterious ways. When we understand this truth, we emerge from a crisis stronger than ever. For Shelley and me, our crisis gave us strength. When we look at the struggles, problems, setbacks, and concerns we've had in our lives, we see the strength we've gained from each one. We believe we can get through anything because we rely on God for His strength. Through that belief, we have hope, and there's nothing we can't handle.

We can't resolve our problems in a moment's time, or take away hurt in an instant. We can't change what happens to us, and we can't change the people in our lives, but we can work on ourselves—we can view every experience as an opportunity. Better yet, we can allow God to work in us, and He will help us become who we are meant to be.

When I'm in a crisis, I pray that I will recognize what I need to learn. What is it that God wants to teach me? I pray, "God, help me to see what you want me to see. Help me understand in this moment." The longer I fight or work against the crisis, the longer I stay there. I want to learn as quickly as possible so I can move out of the crisis moment in a healthy and positive way.

Life-altering events might seem insurmountable. It may feel impossible to see or recognize any opportunity in them. However, we can make the choice to embrace a new mindset, take those first steps forward, and move into our future. What happens externally affects us internally, and difficult circumstances bring the opportunity for internal reflection.

CHAPTER FIVE

CHOOSING DESTINY IN THE MOMENT

The value of life lies not in the length of days, but in the use we make of them.

—MICHEL EYQUEM DE MONTAIGNE

The path of least resistance is rarely the way to reach our destiny. We must face our challenges rather than look for the easy way out. Life presents many obstacles that can prevent us from recognizing our pivot moments, and we keep looking at the past, the could-have-beens, or thinking we've thrown away our future. When we find ourselves unable to move away from a particular thought or feeling or a past or present situation, we have a condition I call "stuckitis."

The *Cambridge Dictionary* defines the word "stuck" as unable to move from a particular place or position, or unable to change a situation. Then, I add four letters, "itis," to make it sound more intense, like an illness. Stuckitis is the condition of being stuck in a particular place, unable to change, and unable to move forward.

Stuckitis varies from person to person and from circumstance to circumstance, but generally speaking, the symptoms include procrastination, avoidance, situational depression, hopelessness, helplessness, and frustration. There is nothing worse than being stuck in a situation that is uncomfortable or even painful. So, how do we deal with stuckitis?

One of my all-time favorite movies is *Dead Poets Society*. Robin Williams's character, John Keating, teaches a class of teenage boys who are caught in groupthink. They think the same way and approach life in the same manner, without giving thought to the other possibilities that might exist. In a memorable scene, Keating climbs up on top of his desk and says, "Why do I stand up here? I stand up here to remind myself that we must constantly look at things in a different way." Keating goes on to quote Thoreau, who said, "Most men lead lives of quiet desperation." Then he adds his own words: "Don't be resigned to that. Break out!"

In other words, change your perspective! Change the way you look at a present problem or difficult circumstance. Changing your perspective and looking at the world in a different way is one way to cure stuckitis. One of the ways to change your perspective is to begin to view your life—both present and future—through eyes of faith.

At some point in life, everyone experiences a form of stuckitis. We get stuck in our careers, family life, or other relationships. We all feel stuck at one point or another, but we don't have to stay there. To get "unstuck," we have to recognize an obstacle, ask a different set of questions, and change our perspective.

When I experience stuckitis, I constantly need to remind myself not to take the easy way out. I need to work hard and put forth the effort to make the necessary changes. It's similar to the work we have to put in to get into good physical shape. Contrary to popular belief, there's no magic pill to get fit. Attempting to get into shape as quickly as possible is an unhealthy approach, and it never leads to true success. It takes work and discipline to get physically fit, and the same is true for our lives and our futures. If we decide to take the easy road with our relationships, careers, marriages, and children, none will thrive—and some will even fail.

REWARD IN THE SACRIFICE

It's much easier to coast downhill than it is to climb a mountain; but to move forward in life, we must pursue the climb. We have to push past the tendency to choose ease and comfort. The best things in life are found just beyond our comfort zones. If we only deal with adversity in the easiest way possible, that mindset defines our future, and we won't make any progress—that choice keeps us in a place where we can't grow.

Growth doesn't happen by chance—it happens by change. Growth only occurs when we're willing to push ourselves out of our comfort zones and intentionally strive for more. Unfortunately, many people don't want to fight the fight. They settle for mediocrity and average results. We'll always face problems and battles in our lives, and when we choose to deny or ignore them, we are choosing defeat. We can't continue to deal with our problems in this manner. The reward is much greater when we embrace the fight and make a determined decision to break out of stuckitis.

Once again, the story of David provides an excellent example for us. The battle with the Philistines wasn't David's fight—he wasn't enlisted in the Israelite army. He would be affected by the outcome of the battle, but he wasn't required to put himself in harm's way. However, 1 Samuel 17:48 tells us, "David ran quickly" to meet

Goliath (NIV). And once he was there, he didn't settle for comfort. He believed in the God he served, and he fought courageously. He knew there was something beyond what he could see in the moment, and he understood that he had to seize the future.

SEIZE YOUR FUTURE

A bright and successful future doesn't just happen by chance. We have to seize it and run quickly to our destiny. If we simply allow things to happen to us, we won't get far, and we certainly won't experience the richness of life. Life is filled with challenges, trials, and stresses, but we don't face life alone—God is with us. It was David's faith that pushed him to do his best. He trusted that God was at his side and would give him success. His faith in God pushed him to not lose hope or courage, even when circumstances seemed impossible. By faith, David took a sling as his weapon, the one he knew very well. Then, he carefully chose the stones he would use and went out to seize the future God had planned. The people who experience richness in life and do great things for God are the ones who are willing to fight for their future. They don't sit back and let life happen; they go out and seize it!

The future holds amazing opportunities and divine moments for all of us, but we must run and take hold of them. Jeremiah 29:11 tells us what God has in store for our lives. "'For I know the plans I have for you,' says the Lord. 'They are plans for good and not for disaster, to give you a future and a hope'" (NLT). We all have a God-given future, but we also have a choice in the matter. We have to *choose* God's plan. God doesn't force us to accept or do His will.

A MASTER PLAN

Life coaching and life planning are big businesses these days, and I'm a strong proponent of both, as I'll discuss in Chapter 7. Today, you can hire a life coach who will help you develop a master plan for your life—that plan will generally include a personal mission statement, as well as one-year and five-year goals. You can even set goals you'd like to reach by the end of your life. These goals are generally related to spiritual, physical, financial, and family matters.

Once you set your goals, your coach will help you develop a specific strategy for reaching them. In other words, you work together to write a description of where you want to be in life within a specified time frame.

The reality is, even if you don't have a formal master plan written for your life, you have one in your head. We all do. We've all imagined what our future looks like. I don't have a written plan, but I certainly have goals and things I want to accomplish. I want to attain a certain level of income and stability for myself and my family. I have goals pertaining to retirement and personal growth. I want my life to matter!

Don't get me wrong; I like making plans. Without them, nothing of value gets accomplished. The Bible has a lot to say about plans. For example, Proverbs 21:5 says, "The plans of the diligent lead surely to abundance, but everyone who is hasty comes only to poverty" (ESV).

But the reality is, there are times when God "messes up" our life plans. God certainly messed up mine, and boy am I glad He did! I never dreamed I'd be the pastor of a large congregation, help start a ministry to serve orphans in Kenya, obtain advanced degrees, or even write this book. That was not part of my plan, but it was in God's plan. He did for me what I never could have accomplished on my own. My plans were faithless and weak compared to what God had in store. Of course, I still have goals, but I want to make sure I'm obedient to God's plan and purpose for my life and family. I often remind myself that even when He calls me to travel a hard road, His plan is always greater than mine.

One of my favorite pictures was taken the night I was ordained. It's of me kneeling at the altar, waiting for the bishop to place his hands on my head and ordain me as an elder in the United Methodist Church. Friends and family gathered around me, but in that moment, I was looking over my shoulder and smiling at my wife, Shelley. In that moment, I was reminded of all the sacrifices we had made to be there. I remembered long nights in the library writing papers for seminary. I remembered giving up time with my family to finish a project. I remembered moving our family multiple times and Shelley driving long distances to work. She carried our whole family on her shoulders so I could finish my doctoral work and meet the requirements for ordination. She was always there to encourage and push me forward.

My wife and I have always been a team, and to this day she still pushes me to work harder, go farther, and try for more. I believe God put her in my life for that very reason. We could have taken the easy path, but we believed that God was calling us to do more. Even when it looked like a situation wasn't going to work or we encountered hard times, we took a step of faith and God honored those steps. God can take what looks impossible and make it possible, but He requires us to move forward and take a step of faith.

David had to take a great step of faith. He was meant to fight that particular battle against Goliath—God positioned him in those circumstances. David's plan was in place and it included the children of Israel, but it was up to David to seize the opportunity. Everyone thought David was crazy for being confident; they didn't believe he had any chance of winning. So, how could David believe it? David said, "The Lord who rescued me from the paw of the lion and the paw of the bear will rescue me from the hand of this Philistine" (1 Samuel 17:37 NIV). David's faith wasn't in himself—his faith was in God. He was confident because he believed that God was with him.

BLESSINGS CONCEALED IN HARDSHIPS

In life's most difficult seasons there's always a blessing. During times of hardship, I've often looked ahead and thought, "This is impossible. I can't win; this is the end." But when I dismissed those thoughts and moved forward, God always seemed to open a door. Not every step of faith was effective—sometimes I took steps in the wrong direction and had to change course—but in the midst of difficulty, I kept moving. You have to keep moving as well.

JACK'S STORY

I have a Kenyan friend named Jack Odhiambo. Jack experienced a life-altering accident while trying to climb aboard a moving train when he was twenty-one years old. He has little recollection of the traumatic event. All he remembers is waking up in a hospital room to find that both of his arms were gone. Jack had fallen on the train track and his arms had been severed by the train's wheels.

Reflecting on the accident, Jack said, "For so long, I wished that I had died under the wheels of that train. In an instant, I went from being a tough street boy to being a baby to people. I had to depend on people to do everything for me. Every night, I would cry to God to be dead."

Jack's future seemed hopeless. He was living on the streets, and he spent every day just trying to survive. His situation would get worse over time, until one day he met a man named Moses at a shelter in Nairobi. Moses encouraged Jack to leave the streets and live in the Christ Compassion Rehabilitation Center, an orphanage in Joska. At the orphanage, Jack was introduced to volunteers from 410 Bridge (www.410Bridge.org), a mission organization from the United States that raised money to get him medical help and to have him fitted with prosthetic arms.

Jack's prosthetic arms gave him a new lease on life, and he believed that God had given him a second chance. He said, "My dream is to be able to share my story of redemption. The biggest lesson I have learned is that no matter what I go through, God has a plan, and He will never leave me."

When confronted with the uncertainties and tragedies

of life, we can see ourselves most clearly. Through Jack's tragedy, God began to reveal to him a greater plan for his life—a plan to go to seminary and become a pastor. He graduated from Bible college, and now people all around the world know him as "Pastor Jack."

When you are at a crossroads in your life and are forced to face your trials and tribulations, or when it seems as if all is lost, put your faith in God to see you through. Part of being human is experiencing both the mountaintop and the valley, and every one of us will have to walk through seasons in the valley. It's the place where life is challenging, where we struggle, and where our battles are fought. In Psalm 23, David speaks of a deep, dark valley where there seems to be no light at the end of the tunnel, nor ray of hope for the future. But valleys are not dead ends. The disappointments, frustrations, discouragements, and dilemmas we face don't define our futures. The valley is the route we all must take to reach our personal promised land—there are no alternative routes. David wrote, "Even though I walk through the darkest valley..." (Psalm 23:4 NIV). Notice that he didn't stay there. He walked through it.

When we take steps forward and dedicate our lives to following the Lord, He provides. I've witnessed many such experiences: He sends the right people at the right time, to do the right things. Through difficult times and through pain, God works things for our good if we choose to believe His promises.

THE TREMENDOUS POWER OF FAITH

Movement in faith requires movement in life. Saying, "I have faith," without making a move, won't get you anywhere. We can talk about faith all day long but real faith requires action. If your faith keeps you in your comfort zone, then it's counterproductive, and probably not real faith. Faith is a verb, not a noun. Faith calls us forward. Faith moves us past obstacles and through seasons of life when we don't have all the answers.

Saul and the Israelites sat in their tents, immobilized by their fear, anxiety, and the very sight of the giant standing in their way. But if you think about it, not one single soldier of the people of Israel had been defeated in battle by Goliath, because not one single soldier had ever *faced* Goliath. They weren't afraid because of past experiences or what the giant had done to them; they were afraid simply because he was *there*! The same is often true for us. We have giants in front of us and they keep us from embracing our moments and going after our God-given dreams. Goliath didn't win by his great faith, his strength, the size of his sword, or how far he could throw his spear—He won because others feared him. Don't let fear rob you of faith and thus keep you from your destiny.

Someone once said that faith is like calories: you can't see them, but you can see their results. There's a lot of truth to that statement. You can't see faith, but you can see its results. That's especially true when you find yourself in a challenging situation. During those seasons, you need to put your faith in God and move forward. Putting your faith in God may seem like risky business. In fact, it can be downright scary at times, but it's a requirement for seizing your future.

Philippians 4:19 tells us, "And my God will meet all your needs according to the riches of his glory in Christ Jesus" (NIV). The easy road is comfortable, and when we're on it, we don't need faith. We need faith when we find ourselves standing before the Goliaths in our lives.

Every day, we have countless opportunities to take the easiest, yet least satisfying, road. We can choose comfort and justify the path of least resistance or we can seize our moment, face our Goliaths, and move toward God's rich destiny for our lives. The choice is ours.

FIGHTING THE BATTLE

When we face times of struggle, we must fight through them. There will be tough choices and circumstances that require resilience. But what does it look like to truly fight the battle?

In the movie *Braveheart*, Mel Gibson's character, warrior-leader William Wallace, rides up and down the front lines of the Scottish army, challenging them to fight the English. The army is made up of common men and farmers—not warriors. None of them wants to fight the enemy for the land and their freedom because they don't want to die on the battlefield.

In one of the most memorable moments of the movie, Wallace says, "Yes, fight and you may die. Run and you will live, at least for a while. And dying in your bed many years from now, would you be willing to trade all the days from this day to that, for one chance, just one chance, to come back here as young men and tell our enemies that they may take our lives, but they will never take our freedom!"

This quote reminds me of how we can become slaves to our circumstances and fears, and that takes life away from us. It can steal our joy, and we may never become the person God intends for us to be. One of my greatest fears is that one day I will look back on my life and realize I missed a moment. I missed an opportunity because I wasn't willing to fight or I didn't have the courage when it counted.

I encourage you to fight, take up the challenge, and move forward. Our greatest moments are often hidden in our most difficult circumstances. When we choose to fight for our future and what's important to us, it can change our destiny forever.

CHAPTER SIX

THE INTERNAL PIVOT

In order to be free, we must learn how to let go. Release the hurt. Release the fear. Refuse to entertain the old pain.

—MARY MANIN MORRISSEY

Internal pivot moments occur when we realize an important truth in our hearts: our lives can be different. We may be down during a tough time, but that doesn't mean we're out!

When we suffer from stuckitis or circular thinking, we can't see past the issue in front of us. We go around and around, asking if we're doing enough, and that's the wrong question—it's inherently negative.

SIGNS OF CIRCULAR THINKING

Some of us may be stuck in a pattern of circular thinking and not even know it. Examine the following list of tendencies and answer these questions honestly:

Mood swings—Do your thoughts create negative emotions and actions?

Focus on past problems and future events—Do you attempt to escape your present circumstances by thinking of past successes? Do you look to future events with the expectation that they will make you happy?

Judgment—Are you highly judgmental of yourself and others?

Destructive habits—Do you drink excessively or engage in other harmful, unproductive activities?

Anxiety and worry—Are these emotions dominant in your life?

If you can identify with one or more of these emotions, thoughts, or actions, you may be stuck in circular thinking. If you are, how do you regain your composure and stop the downward spiral? You must change the way you think. You know you've fallen into a circular thinking pattern when you find yourself using words like "can't," "always," and "never." "I can't get over it." "This always happens to me." "I'll never pay off this debt." Those words alone create a mindset of defeat.

Remember the snowball effect from Chapter 2? Negative thoughts gain momentum in circular thinking—they build on one another. As these thoughts continue, they develop a distorted picture of reality. Worry, anxiety, and fear can intensify these negative thoughts, sending us into a brutal downward spiral.

Oftentimes, aspects of the arguments in our mind are logically valid, so if the premises can be true, we think the conclusions must be true. These negative thoughts, emotions, and behaviors form a vicious feedback loop. For example, you get a bad review from your boss and it's upsetting. The negative emotions bring negative possibilities in your mind, and you begin thinking of other mistakes you've made at your job. Then, you picture yourself getting fired, moving in with your parents, and maybe even living on the streets!

THE BATTLE IN OUR MINDS

The most intense battle many of us will fight in difficult times is the one in our minds. If we can win this battle, we can do anything! King Solomon, who quite possibly was the wisest man who ever lived, warns us about this battle in Proverbs 23:7: "Be careful how you think; your life is shaped by your thoughts" (GNT).

This is a simple yet powerful statement. Your thoughts determine your actions. Actions determine your habits. Habits determine your character, and character always determines your destiny. To break the pattern of circular thinking and reach the destiny God has for you, start replacing the negative words "can't," "always," and "never" with statements of truth.

We have a spiritual enemy, and his greatest desire is to knock us off course and prevent us from living the full, rich lives God has planned for us. In 2 Corinthians 10:5, we are instructed to "demolish arguments and every pretension that sets itself up against the knowledge of God, and...take captive every thought to make it obedient to Christ" (NIV). We get to choose what we think about, and rather than giving the enemy control, we must allow God to transform our thoughts.

I can't stress enough the importance of taking your thoughts captive. To emerge from the battle in victory, you must "think about what you think about." In Romans 12:2, Paul says, "Don't copy the behavior and customs of this world, but let God transform you into a new person by changing the way you think. Then you will learn to know God's will for you, which is good and pleasing and perfect" (NLT).

In John 8:44, Jesus calls the devil "the father of lies and of all that is false" (AMPC). We can't believe the lies he tells us about our circumstances and ourselves. We must acknowledge negative and destructive thoughts and replace them with truth.

PIVOT YOUR FOCUS

We know that King David had many troubled seasons in his life. He was lonely, afraid, and depressed. One such time was when he returned home to Ziklag after a long journey and discovered that his enemies, the Amalekites, had stolen everything that was important to him. His family and the families of his men had been taken captive. As David sat among the burned ruins of Ziklag while his men threatened to stone him, David had a choice to make. He could let the grief and sadness overtake him and be defeated by his circumstances, or he could fight back.

David's first battle wasn't a physical battle—he had to fight the one taking place in his mind. He had to look beyond his present circumstances. Instead of focusing on his problems, he focused on the Lord. In 1 Samuel 30:6, we see David redirecting his thoughts toward God: "And David was greatly distressed; for the people spake of stoning him, because the soul of all the people was grieved, every man for his sons and for his daughters: but David encouraged himself in the Lord his God" (KJV).

David's circumstances were discouraging, to say the least, and if David had continued to focus on the situation, defeat would have been inevitable. But David chose to encourage himself in God. Why? Because he knew God was the constant force in his life. No matter David's circumstances, whether fighting Goliath or the Amalekites, he turned to the never-changing, eternal God, the One who is above our circumstances and able to see us through whatever we face in life.

When we are distressed and life feels out of control, we must do as David did. We can't let ourselves fall into fear, anxiety, and worry. We should encourage ourselves in the Lord, our God, and fight the battle in our minds!

INTERNAL PIVOTS IN ACTION

A good friend of mine is a high-performing CEO of a Fortune 500 Company. She works long, stressful days— twelve to fourteen hours is the norm. Due to her heavy workload, her level of responsibility, and the stress of her job, she found herself unable to fall asleep at night. So, in order to "wind down" from a busy day and rest, she began having a few drinks in the evenings.

She started out just having a drink here and there for relaxation, but eventually she developed the habit of consuming several drinks each night to fall asleep. She believed she could not rest without it, and alcohol became a part of her everyday life.

To her credit, my friend had the strength and awareness to realize she had developed an addiction to alcohol. She recognized her dependence on it and the lie she had told herself—that she couldn't fall sleep without having a few drinks. She replaced that lie with the truth and instead told herself, "I don't need alcohol to sleep. I don't need it to get through the day." She fought the battle over alcohol in her mind and won. Today, she no longer has the desire for alcohol and she doesn't need it as a crutch to fall asleep. It was a daily fight for her to move away from alcohol, but she found victory through counseling and by connecting to a support-group community that held her accountable.

GOD IS ENOUGH

The National Institute of Mental Health cites depression as the number-one mental health problem in the United States, with hospital bills and medications to treat the condition costing billions of dollars annually. Discouragement and depression can happen to anyone, even to the best and strongest people. Martin Luther battled severe bouts of depression at times, and many pastors today struggle with burnout and feelings of inadequacy.

I have a colleague who is an outstanding pastor and leads

a vibrant ministry in the Metro Atlanta area. His church has grown significantly over the years, and many people testify that he led them to God or helped strengthen their relationship with Him. However, he never felt he was doing enough and was often overcome with feelings of inadequacy. He attended conferences, read books, and viewed webinars to improve his leadership and communication skills. Even though lifelong learning is an important part of a pastor's life, his motivation for it came from fear. He didn't want that suffocating, paralyzing feeling of inadequacy to overtake him.

We began spending time together and talking over coffee. He shared many stories about his years in ministry and talked about the incredible things God had done in his life. It was hard to believe he was struggling to keep his sense of self-worth above water. He was constantly worried about having enough time to prepare his messages, lead his growing congregation, and meet all of his pastoral duties. He was truly overwhelmed and it was beginning to affect his marriage.

Over the next year, my ministry friend sought help from a counselor/coach to deal with his feelings. We still got together for coffee from time to time, and it was amazing to see the transformation that took place in his life. Eventually, he replaced the lie of "I'm not enough" with "God is enough." He realized God was using him in wonderful ways, and He had equipped him with everything he needed. He is now confident that he has the knowledge, skill, and ability to do what God has called him to do.

BREAKING FREE

A member of one of my previous congregations is another testament to resilience and faith. Through a series of incidents and life decisions, she developed an addiction to crystal meth. Her husband was a user, and together they started using the drug recreationally. Crystal meth is strong and highly addictive, and it wasn't long before she was using it every day.

The drug destroyed her marriage, but she was unwilling to take responsibility for her actions. Her days were consumed with negative thoughts, like, "Why did I choose the wrong partner?" and "Why did I marry so young?" She wanted to go back in time to undo the experience, but she couldn't. She had to move past that longing and accept that addiction was the real problem.

Unable to come to grips with the real problems in her life, she began to spiral downward. She lost her job, her home, and her family. She was left without the resources to pay for her addiction, so she turned to prostitution for a time to fund her habit. She tried to make a change many times, but the addiction had too strong of a grip on her. She was unable to make her own decisions—the addiction made them for her.

Her pivot moment occurred when she hit rock bottom. Completely overwhelmed by guilt and shame, she stopped making excuses for her addiction. She admitted that it had complete control over her life and she needed help.

She began taking steps toward recovery and reconciliation. She called her family and they led her to a rehab facility. She met with addiction and psychological counselors, and she continued to take courageous steps toward rebuilding her life.

Soon after she had completed the treatment program, she came to the church. We talked, and she told me that through the course of her counseling, she came to understand the lies she had internalized. When she was growing up, her mother was verbally abusive and critical of everything she did. She had internalized these words, and in turn they had shaped her identity. She believed she would never be good enough. She thought, "I'll never be good enough for my family. I'll never be a good enough mother for my children. There's no one who will ever truly love me."

She realized those words were lies and came to see the

truth. Once she could see who she was in God's eyes, she made incredible changes. It was a lengthy process, but she knew she had a future. She is now married to a man who knows everything about her past, and he loves and accepts her completely. She's restoring her relationship with her children and continuing to move forward in life.

THE THIEF IN THE STRUGGLE

In all of these examples, poor decisions and negative thoughts were rooted in past life experiences—a false belief manifested in an external issue. We can see the ways in which the spiritual adversary in the world uses these lies to try to destroy us. He attempts to steal who we are and what we can be. When our identity is stolen, we believe things about ourselves that are untrue. We identify with negative thoughts and not with who we are in Christ.

A false identity is never a good one; it's not the one that gives us hope and a future. It leads us to make decisions based on lies, and those lies are not in God's Word or plan. When the people in the previous stories replaced lies with the truth, they were able to pivot and change direction.

In John 10:10, Jesus says, "The thief comes only to steal and kill and destroy" (ESV). The killing is not a physical death but a spiritual death in our minds. We need to remember that a mistake, failure, or shortcoming is a temporary event; it does not define who we are. We begin to die spiritually when we allow these events to define us.

Sometimes, there is a long-term price to pay for choices we've made, but we always have hope. What happens internally influences external processes. When I change the way I think, it changes the way I act. What goes on inside of me becomes what takes place around me—it's the physical manifestation of reaping and sowing.

CHAPTER SEVEN

NAVIGATING THE PIVOT

What you get by reaching your goals is not nearly so important as what you become by reaching them.

—ZIG ZIGLAR

At this point, I hope you've reached an important milestone in your life—a crossroads where you've decided to pivot in the direction of a bright future. So, where do you go from here? How do you find and reach the solutions to your problems?

THREE TOOLS OF PIVOT NAVIGATION

Making pivot changes alone can be difficult. Fortunately, there are three valuable tools that can help you through the process: a coach, a community, and new priorities.

THE IMPORTANCE OF A COACH

When you are ready to move forward, it's beneficial to ask someone to walk the path with you. It's tremendously empowering to have someone share ideas and help you work through your challenges. For that reason, I always sought out a coach (or mentor)—someone to hold me accountable for my decisions and goals. My coach called me out when I made excuses, kept me focused on moving forward, and wouldn't let me take the easy way out.

I've had a coach during both good and bad times, and my experiences with them have always been successful. Consider the coaches for professional golfers or Olympic athletes. They don't just coach when the athlete is doing something wrong; a good coach helps them to grow and develop their skills, keeps them focused to the finish, and holds them accountable to a plan.

Christian versus Secular Coaching

As a Christian pastor, I believe the best life coaches are Christian life coaches. Think about it: Jesus Christ was the ultimate life coach! In the Gospel of John, Jesus said, "The thief comes only to steal and kill and destroy. I came that [you] may have life and have it abundantly" (John 10:10 ESV). There are similarities between Christian and secular life coaches, but there is one unique and very important distinction: a Christian life coach offers advice through the lens of a biblical worldview. They can help you discover your purpose in life and show you how to walk in your destiny, gain fresh perspective on personal challenges and opportunities, demolish mindsets that hold you back, improve your relationships, develop a plan of action, and learn how to hear God's voice in the process.

Secular coaching challenges you to look within yourself and listen to what your heart is telling you; they encourage you to focus on your inner strengths and go with what feels right. There is no absolute truth from this perspective. There are also no boundaries and few rules, and God is not involved in the process. This brings to mind Proverbs 14:12, which states, "There is a way that appears to be right, but in the end it leads to death" (NIV).

Christian life coaching is centered in the knowledge that you were created in the image of God, and therefore, He has a plan for your life. You were not an accident; you were not thrown together, nor were you some cosmic mistake. The Bible teaches that you were created in the *very image of God.*

Genesis 1:26 states, "Then God said, 'Let us make human beings in our image, to be like us'" (NLT). This is the one thing that makes humans different from every other created animal. This is what makes humanity so unique.

When God created you, He got His hands dirty! The word for "image" comes from the Hebrew word *tselem*, which refers to carving. It is the idea that humanity was carved into the very shape and image of God.

You are extremely important to God because you bear His likeness—that's not true for the rest of creation. The heavens may declare the glory of God, the vastness of the galaxies may reveal His greatness, and the mountains and the oceans may display His beauty, but only humanity reflects the image of God. HeGod was intentional in creation, and everything He created has a purpose. Therefore, He has a plan and purpose for your life, and you need to know what they are in order to move forward.

Freedom through Christian Coaching

Take a moment to ponder the fact that God knows everything about you. There is not a single aspect of your life that God is not fully aware of! Both the good and the bad experiences in your life are already completely known by God. Psalm 139:13 says, "For you created my inmost being; you knit me together in my mother's womb" (NIV).

God knows what makes you tick. God knows what gives you joy, and He knows your greatest fears. Therefore, it is vitally important to invite God to be a part of the coaching process. Christian life coaches will come alongside you to support, encourage, and challenge you to become all that God has created you to be, do, and become. One of the greatest moments of my life came when a coach helped me to clearly see how some of my beliefs about myself were negatively affecting me; they were keeping me from reaching my God-given potential.

This coach led me to see that I was a perfectionist—I lived my life running on a terrible treadmill, thinking I had to be perfect. My perfectionism didn't manifest itself in a meticulously organized closet or junk drawer. It manifested in far more self-defeating ways. For example, I was so petrified of failure that I would have trouble completing a project because I thought there was always something I could do to make it better. To make matters worse, my self-confidence and self-worth depended on my accomplishments and what other people thought about my work. I strived for excellence and needed the validation from other people to feel good about myself—the belief that I had to be perfect caused a lot of anxiety and pain in my life. Therefore, I procrastinated or avoided situations where I couldn't excel. Psychologists say procrastinators are actually perfectionists at heart!

It was liberating to me when my coach helped me to see that this mindset and behavior was affecting my professional life and stunting my spiritual growth. Even though perfectionism still rears its ugly head from time to time,

I can recognize it and work through it. Now I understand that hard work and striving for excellence is a positive quality, but it can have a negative impact when it defines my life and becomes the method for personal validation.

Humans are not perfect, and we will make mistakes! These mistakes can become pivot moments when we choose to learn from them and move forward.

EMBRACE YOUR COMMUNITY

In his book *Bowling Alone*, Robert Putnam says the greatest social epidemic in America is loneliness. We all know people who go home every night, grab snacks, and binge on Netflix—they live an isolated existence and it's not healthy.

When life feels difficult or we experience a crisis, our natural inclination is to get away from other people and be alone, when, in fact, we need to do the opposite. When we feel lonely, depressed, or alienated from family and friends, we need to find a community and change our environment.

It's important to pursue a community and be with people. God created us in and for a relationship. That is why when God created the first human, He immediately said, "It is not good for man to be alone" (Genesis 2:18 DRA). We were not designed to live alone—we were meant to live in community and it should be an integral part of our lives.

God himself is community—the Father, Son, and Holy Spirit. In Paul Tripp's book *Whiter Than Snow: Meditations on Sin and Mercy*, he says we were not created to be independent, autonomous, or self-sufficient. We were made to live in a humble, worshipful, loving dependency on God, and in a loving and humble interdependency with others.

We were designed to live in community. Unfortunately, when we are in the midst of a crisis season, our first reaction is to isolate ourselves from others. We often think we have all we need within ourselves. Even when life is good, we settle for casual relationships and don't truly connect with others. We defend ourselves when people shine a light on our weaknesses or mistakes. We don't take advantage of the God-given resource of community.

Strength in Numbers

A few years ago, I spent some time in Kenya, in eastern Africa. While I was there, I had the opportunity to go on a safari in the Maasai Mara National Reserve. It was an incredible experience, as I viewed one majestic scene after another, and our group saw a lion pride attack a single water buffalo. We learned that the pride works together to separate their selected prey from the herd and they move in for the kill once it's isolated.

This illustration isn't just true in the animal kingdom; it also applies to humans. When we reject community and choose to remain alone, we are vulnerable—defeatist attitudes, depression, fear, and destructive behavior can take control of our lives. This is why it's important to find a community, especially when we're in difficult circumstances.

CREATE NEW PRIORITIES

Developing new priorities and routines is an important part of making positive changes in your life. In fact, a change in routine can cause a change in how you see the world. Our actions determine outcomes, and they also demonstrate our attitude toward the world around us. Creating new priorities requires that we create a new vision for our lives. It requires that we see ourselves, not as we are, but as we could be.

Professor Samuel Mockbee was the visionary behind the Rural Studio, an architectural firm that specializes in making unique, functional, low-cost public buildings and homes for poor residents in Alabama. Mockbee and his students make these unique, functional buildings out of trash—they turn scrap building materials, old car parts, used tires, and other pieces of rubbish into real homes.

Some of his students used these materials to build a chapel and community center for the residents of Mason's Bend, a small town in rural Alabama. The students used more than one hundred discarded car windows to make one of the walls for the center. Other students used seventy-two thousand individually stacked carpet tiles to construct insulated walls for a home. Some of the homes they've built are so attractive, they've been featured in architectural magazines!

There is great genius behind their architecture—they create value in things that seemingly have no value, and they see potential in things that others see as useless. They see these things not as they are but as what they could become. Some people look at discarded car windows and see trash, and others see building materials. The difference is in their *vision*.

When you look at your life, what do you see? Can you see beyond your present circumstances? Can you envision yourself in a different place? How you look at your world and how you look at yourself determines, to a great extent, who you will be in the future.

Leave Regrets Behind

I might be bummed out by the way my favorite football team's season ended, but I don't *regret* it. I don't have regret because I had no power over the outcome. However, when an outcome is in our control and we make the wrong decision, we can get bogged down in a sea of regrets. We despair about decisions we did (or didn't) make. All pain stings, but regret has a unique sting because it goes beyond the thought, "I wish things had turned out differently." You *know* things could have turned out differently if you had made another choice, and that makes regret harder to bear than any other form of disappointment.

Sometimes, we are afraid to move forward because we fear we will make a mistake or mess up. At times, I'm plagued with the bad habit of focusing on the worst possible outcomes of making a decision, instead of an opportunity that is before me—this is because of a fear of failure. But I've come to realize that there are worse things in life than failure.

Several years ago, we gave my son Robert a remote-control helicopter as a Christmas gift. He immediately wanted to fly the helicopter in our yard. Unfortunately, I knew we couldn't fly it successfully—our yard wasn't big enough and it was filled with a number of large oak trees. Therefore, the helicopter sat on a shelf in his room for months.

Almost daily, Robert begged me to take him into the yard

and fly it. Every time he asked, I reminded him that our yard was full of trees and it would inevitably get stuck in one of them. Eventually, he wore me down and in a weak, somewhat-aggravated moment I decided to let him fly it. As you can imagine, a few short minutes into our helicopter flying adventure, he flew it into the largest tree in our yard. I thought for sure he was going to be crushed, but instead he just laughed, gave me a fist bump, and talked about how much fun it was.

What I thought was going to be a great lesson for him turned out to be a lesson for me! Remnants of that helicopter are still in the tree, and every time I see them I'm reminded of this truth: it's better to fly a helicopter and get it stuck in a tree than to never fly it at all. Remember this: every opportunity has an expiration date, and the cost of missing out can be greater than the cost of messing up. Success happens when you choose to work through life's failures and regrets, and grow from your mistakes.

You've probably heard the saying "Yesterday is history, tomorrow is a mystery, but today is a gift. That is why it is called 'the present.'" You've been given the wonderful gift of this present moment. In this moment, you have the ability to develop a new vision, create new priorities for your life, and change your circumstances. You can pivot!

JUMP-START YOUR DAY

The culmination of our days ultimately determines who we become and our success in life. Therefore, how you start your day has a profound influence on its success.

There were days early in my faith journey when I'd wake up, crawl out of bed, make myself a cup of coffee, and then turn on the television to watch the news while I got dressed. It didn't take me long to realize that the images I saw and the words I heard had a major influence over my entire day. Many times, those influences created a negative trajectory for my day—they affected my view of the world and my life overall. However, over time I began to understand that I could change the direction of my day by changing what I allowed to influence my mornings. Now, I make the choice to invest in my relationship with God at the beginning of each day.

The Bible makes it clear that spending time with God should be a priority in our lives.

Psalm 143:8 says, "Let the morning bring me word of your unfailing love, for I have put my trust in you. Show me the way I should go, for to you I entrust my life" (NIV).

Paul also explains the importance of spending time with God in 2 Corinthians 4:6. He writes, "For God, who said, 'Let there be light in the darkness,' has made this light shine in our hearts so we could know the glory of God that is seen in the face of Jesus Christ" (NLT).

When God's light shines in our hearts, we begin to know His fullness. As we get to know Him better, we begin to understand the magnitude of His love and grace for us, found in Jesus Christ. When we see ourselves through the lens of Christ, our lives begin to make sense—we gain a greater understanding of who God created us to be. And it's this understanding of God that gives us the ability to look to the future, knowing that God's redemptive power is at work. We can be confident that we have a purpose in God's plan.

Spending time with God in the mornings contributed to the pivot moment in my life, but I didn't develop the discipline to do it overnight. Creating the habit of daily devotional time takes practice, and getting started can be the hardest part. If the idea of a daily devotion is a new concept for you, I'd like to share my morning routine to help you get started.

MY MORNING ROUTINE

When I wake up in the morning, I (1) pray, (2) read my Bible and/or a devotional, and then (3) journal my thoughts. This pattern has had a profound impact on my life!

Prayer (Five Minutes)

I spend the first five minutes of my day praying. Prayer gives us the opportunity to share every aspect of our lives with God. Although it may seem difficult at first, your prayer time can become one of the most powerful moments of your day. Over the years, many people have told me that they "don't know how to pray," but this simply isn't true for anyone—prayer is nothing more than talking to God! A simple way to start praying is to thank God for the blessings in your life. Even if you are facing major challenges or setbacks, there is always something to be thankful for.

Prayer also gives us the opportunity to share our concerns with God. The circumstances of our lives change on a daily basis; each day is filled with different challenges to face, problems to solve, and obstacles to maneuver. Whatever your concerns might be, offer them to God. Ask God to give you the wisdom to make right decisions, and the strength to endure each and every circumstance. The Bible offers incredible insight about prayer in Philippians 4:6-7: "Tell God what you need, and thank him for all he has done. Then you will experience God's peace, which exceeds anything we can understand" (NLT). It's been said that prayer doesn't always change our situation, but it always changes us.

Bible Study/Devotional (Ten to Fifteen Minutes)

For the second part of my morning routine, I read and study the Bible. This can be informal or in a structured format, with the use of a study guide or a Bible reading plan. No matter how you do it, the ultimate goal is to get to know God.

Getting closer to God is similar to getting to know a new friend. And how do we get to know someone? By spending time with them! The Bible contains God's words to us, so when we spend time studying the Scriptures and praying, it's like having a conversation with God. So many of life's questions can be answered in the Scriptures. For example, what is the purpose of life? Why is there evil in the world? Why do I struggle to do what is right? Is there life after death? Not only does the Bible answer these questions (and many more), but it also gives us practical advice that we can apply to our daily lives.

Journaling (Ten Minutes)

Another essential part of my time with God is spent journaling. Simply writing down your thoughts and feelings can be one of the most potent and powerful activities you can acquire and can also be one of the most therapeutic activities you can engage in. Journaling can help you process your thoughts and control your emotions when you're dealing with a crisis or struggling with stress, anxiety, and situational depression. It can also help generate clarity of thought and spark your creativity. I can't begin to express the impact that journaling has had on my spiritual life! I'm able to look back at my journal and see answered prayers, and I can reflect upon dark times and see that they were significant in shaping who I am today.

IN SUMMARY

The practices of prayer, reading and studying the Bible, and journaling are essential in my faith. If I start my day without this time with God, I feel as if something is missing—it seems as if the pieces of my life aren't connected. There is not a single practice in my life that has had such a profound, positive effect on every *other* aspect of my life! The little things we do every day can have the greatest impact on our lives and our future. John Ortberg, author of *The Life You've Always Wanted*, says consistent spiritual discipline becomes "a rhythm for living in which we can grow more intimately connected with God."

Getting a jump start on your day will help you live a more focused life. When you start your mornings with the discipline of daily devotional time, you will establish a rhythm for living that leads to success and has a huge impact on your life. My daily time with God has helped me through many difficult times, and it will help you through yours, too! By spending time with God and having faith in Him, we prepare ourselves to face a multitude of different situations in the future.

CHAPTER EIGHT

CRISIS AND PIVOT CREATE MOMENTUM

Progress is impossible without change, and those who cannot change their minds cannot change anything.

—GEORGE BERNARD SHAW

The dynamics of external moments and internal pivots work together to create momentum. By recognizing challenge moments and using faith as your guide, pivot moments lead you to the destiny God has for you. In addition to the positive changes in your own life, others will see your transformation and the miraculous results it brings.

When we experience hardships, we want life to change. However, the desire to change and taking steps toward it are two different things. A true pivot moment occurs when we change our perspective, our attitude, and the way we think; the new perspective allows us to see our present circumstances in a different light.

Choosing the easy way out creates a false pivot moment. Change is difficult, and we can only grow when we are willing to make those changes. One of my favorite quotes says, "Change happens when the pain of staying the same is greater than the pain of change." It begins with the desire to change, a plan of action, and movement toward a desired outcome. Without those three components, real change cannot take place.

THE NEED FOR CHANGE

I have coached many people through difficult times. Some of them, despite their pain, did not feel a desire to change. False pivot moments occur when our actions don't match our desired outcome. To change effectively, you must have the desire and a design. In other words, you've got to want the change to take place at the heart level, and you must have a plan to make it happen. Once those two components are in place, you need to take the first step toward seeing the change come to fruition. I know that first step can be incredibly difficult, and unfortunately, we often hit rock bottom before we are willing to take it.

I once helped a woman in my community who was a severe alcoholic. Due to her drinking, there had been many incidents that affected her four young children. She had been pulled over for drunk driving while she had her kids in the car, she couldn't find her car in a grocery store parking lot, and at times, she forgot to feed her children. A friend once visited her home to discover her six-year-old making soup for her younger siblings because their mother was too intoxicated to make dinner. This family was not down on their luck or struggling financially in any way; they were a middle-class family and their needs were being met. It was a sad situation.

The mother joined me at church to talk about her issues. She cried and was in a great deal of pain. She said she wanted her life to be different, but never took steps to change her actions. She went to rehab several times, but was repeatedly dismissed from the programs because she was unwilling to commit to the process. Her desire to change never lined up with her actions, so the situation never improved.

We are masters of justifying our behavior in our minds. We make excuses, defend ourselves, and try to cover up our faults and failures. We say we can't change for various reasons and we think the excuses justify our actions. The unacceptable becomes acceptable over time as we condition ourselves to negative behaviors. We can't make progress with that mindset. In Romans 7, Paul says he has discovered a principle of life—that mental desire and definitive action are often at odds with one another. "When I want to do what is right, I inevitably do what is wrong. I love God's law with all my heart. But there is another power within me that is at war with my mind. This power makes me a slave to the sin that is still within me. Oh, what a miserable person I am! Who will free me from this life that is dominated by sin and death?" (Romans 7:21–24 NLT).

Paul then tells us the answer is in Jesus Christ. He is the source of freedom, understanding, and the power to make changes. When the mother from the previous story doubted she had the power to make the necessary changes, she was right. She couldn't do it on her own— she needed God to help her.

When we allow God to work in our hearts and His power to work in our lives, there's nothing He can't do in and through us. If we revisit the story of David, we can see he never desired to cause pain, heartache, and death in his family, but his actions gave birth to a host of devastating outcomes. We're often caught in a similar situation. Sin causes pain in our lives and in the lives of others, and we face the consequences. We may think we can't break free of the situation, but God equips us with all we need. It's hard work, but change is possible when we let God work in our lives.

BELIEVE IN YOURSELF AND ACT ON IT

Dr. Bobby Hoffman, an educational psychologist and associate professor at the University of Central Florida, believes most people have little insight into what ignites their daily behavior. Hoffman says what motivates and drives our behavior is implicit self-belief. These beliefs determine what we do, how we do it, and how we see ourselves in relation to the rest of the world. Ironically, if we were asked to identify these beliefs, we'd have no idea what they were, even though they influence our career paths, relationships, and life decisions, and ultimately determine our destinies.

A common question I'm asked as a pastor is, "What is God's will for my life?" I believe this question can cause confusion and struggles for many of us. We want to know all the answers before we find our way. We want to know which direction to go and the reason why things happen. In the midst of these questions, we must understand that attitude and self-belief will motivate our actions, and those actions will determine our destiny.

In theory, having a positive attitude should be easy but it's daunting. More often than not, we need help to change, and the process works best when we allow God to do the heavy lifting in our hearts. There is a distinct connection between where we are today and the choices we've made in the past. It's painful to think that some of the junk we experience now is a result of our own error in judgment, but God offers forgiveness and gives us the ability to change and move forward.

DEMOLISH THE STRONGHOLDS

The most ardent Christians who walk with God still struggle with negative attitudes and behaviors. Some wrestle with fear, anxiety, depression, and destructive behaviors. Paul talks about this in 2 Corinthians 10:3-4: "For though we live in the world, we do not wage war as the world does. The weapons we fight with are not the weapons of the world. On the contrary, they have divine power to demolish strongholds" (NIV).

"Stronghold" is a powerful word. It doesn't matter if you are a Christian or not; everyone can develop strongholds in their minds. A stronghold is a way of thinking or living that serves as a reference point for truth. They take the form of attitudes, mindsets, emotions, philosophies, or teachings that oppose God's Word. They establish themselves in our minds, and it's difficult to move away from them.

Going back to Paul's statement in Romans 12:2, he says, "Let God transform you into a new person by changing the way you think" (NLT). It's critical for us to understand our reference point for truth, because what we believe will shape our lives. We must recognize the false or negative influences in our minds and choose to believe what God says—we need to see His Word as eternal truth. Only then can we tear down strongholds.

In my family, we compare thoughts and statements to God's truth, and we do our best to live our lives based on His Word. We do this when we gather together to pray, do our devotions, and worship. We try to teach this truth to our children so they will understand it and grow in wisdom; we want God's Word to establish their identity and motivate their actions.

We live in a culture that doesn't believe in absolute truth. Everyone has different points of view and unique sets of truths, but God's truth is absolute. His Word does not shift or change to be culturally relevant or politically correct—it moves and transcends from culture to culture, from century to millennia. We should aim to build lives with meaning and purpose, built on the solid foundation of God's eternal truth.

MOMENTUM KILLERS

There are three main strongholds that kill momentum: fear, unforgiveness, and negative self-talk.

FEAR

Some fear is healthy and normal; it's a gift from God that helps us heed warnings and prevents us from making foolish choices. However, the stronghold type of fear is the one that keeps us from moving forward in life—it can paralyze or destroy us. When people suffer from this type of fear, it's not based on reality. It forms when our own sense of security doesn't sustain us.

In today's world, adversity seems to lurk around every corner, so it's natural to feel and maintain a certain level of fear. We can't be sure a marriage will last, that we'll always have a job, or that our family members will always be healthy. Many are afraid to move into their future because they are held in the grip of fear.

UNFORGIVENESS

In Matthew 18:21–22, Peter comes to Jesus and asks, "Lord, how many times shall I forgive my brother or sister who sins against me? Up to seven times?" Jesus answers, "I tell you, not seven times, but seventy-seven times" (NIV).

In Jesus's day, the rabbis taught that a person must forgive three times. Peter thought he was being generous when he said seven times. However, Jesus's response of "seventy-seven times," or in another translation "seventy times seven," means that there is not a numerical limit on the number of times we should forgive. The reason for Jesus's exaggeration is because forgiveness is not for the person who hurt you—forgiveness is for you.

Choosing not to forgive has a devastating effect on our lives. It holds us back from our future. Unforgiveness is an ugly emotion. It's full of resentment, hostility, bitterness, anger, fear, and even hatred. Unforgiveness develops over time, and it can produce destructive effects in our lives. When we harbor unforgiveness, it poisons not only the relationship with the person who hurt us, but it can negatively impact all of our relationships.

For years, I held on to resentment toward my mother. I blamed her for my parents' divorce and the breakup of our family. Looking back, I can see how it negatively impacted some of my most important relationships. Many of us have endured hurtful, difficult situations at the hands of another. Some scenarios are horrific, and I can't even begin to imagine the pain that was inflicted, but we still need to forgive. That said, forgiving someone who hurt you is not easy.

You can forgive a person without reconciling the relationship. You've probably heard the phrase, "forgive and forget." The problem with that statement is that it's not always possible to forget an offense. However, it is possible to forgive the person. We can choose to forgive someone and let go of all the negative emotions we feel toward them without restoring the relationship. We can forgive without reconciling. There may be times when you feel a sense of finality and closure about a relationship, but you do not wish to rebuild it. You may even find that your life is much better and more peaceful because that relationship is not a part of it.

Pastor Charles Swindoll likens unforgiveness to drinking poison and expecting someone else to die. Forgiveness is not for the benefit of the other person—it's for you. In my case, forgiving my mother was the key that unlocked the prison I had been stuck in for so long. Choosing forgiveness released me from bondage.

When we bring circumstances and bitter feelings of the past into the present, it can destroy our future. Had I not forgiven my mother, I most likely would have sabotaged my relationship with Shelley. When we forgive, we make the choice in our hearts not to retaliate. We accept and release the sin of another and we let God handle the rest.

NEGATIVE SELF-TALK

People often ask me which preacher I listen to most often, and I tell them it's me—the guy I look at in the mirror every morning. We have the strongest influence on ourselves and our words have power. Proverbs 18:21 says,

"The tongue has the power of life and death, and those who love it will eat its fruit" (NIV). This doesn't just apply to our relationships with other people; it applies to the words we speak to *ourselves*.

Every word we choose either gives life or brings death. My good friend Pete Wilson says our words are not neutral; every single one has direction. They can move in the direction of hope, love, peace, unity, correction, and wisdom, or they can move toward anger, jealousy, contempt, violence, judgment, and condemnation. The choice is ours.

Ultimately, the words we speak will bear the fruit of our lives so we need to do away with negative talk and replace it with the truth of God's Word. Remember, He did not give us a spirit of fear, but of power, love, and self-control. Through Him we have the ability to forgive those who have wronged us. Following God's Word breaks the strongholds in our lives and keeps us moving forward.

GOD AS THE FOUNDATION

Pivot moments create the desire to change. Along with that desire, we should have a plan of action with steps to move toward that change. When those pieces connect, it develops positive momentum. Everything we think and do sows seeds for our future; positive seeds will reap a positive harvest.

When we work through the fear we have on the inside, it leads to a powerful external change. If our lives are built on faith and not on culture or the negative experiences around us, God becomes the architect for our future. He is the foundation and we can build a mindset of positive influences.

Making positive changes alters the trajectory of our lives. When we find ourselves in dark, ugly, painful moments, we need to assess how we think and act. If it's negative, we must determine a new pattern. As the creative rap pioneer Ice Cube once said, "Check yourself before you wreck yourself."

Embrace the moment, let God lead, and there can be a miracle in your destiny!

AFTERWORD

FROM DARKEST MOMENT TO NEW BEGINNING

There will come a time when you believe everything is finished. That will be the beginning.

—LOUIS L'AMOUR

Times of crisis are seasons, and all seasons come to an end. Every dark moment has light; we just have to search to find it. Recognizing and embracing a pivot moment allows us to break free—we have a new perspective. External circumstances and internal change ignite a powerful charge to create momentum in our lives.

At times, we are so blinded by painful circumstances and fall into negative thought patterns that we think a struggle is going to last forever. However, living your life in a way that creates positive momentum can shorten a difficult season.

Stay true to yourself, lean on God, and don't focus on the past. Don't keep asking, "Why me?" But be careful not to focus too much on the future, either. Being mindful of and planning for the future is important to find your way out of the darkness, but the journey begins when we *embrace the present*. Embracing the moment brings clarity that shows you the light ahead. Pivoting is a two-step process where we must first desire to change and then create a plan to move toward that change.

Living in isolation or thinking you can change on your own won't help you find a new perspective. Even when you're in the shadows, think about where you want to go from there. What do you want out of life? What brings you joy? Don't fall into the trap of thinking you are stuck in your present situation forever. Remember, life isn't ending; it's just beginning.

We all face difficult circumstances in life. We may not know which direction to go; we might lie awake at night, desperate to know there is a plan and a future. It's during those times that we must put our trust in God and remember His greatest promise: He will never leave us or forsake us.

Every situation in life holds an opportunity to pivot. An internal change must take place before you can see external results. Shift your focus to your destiny and where you want to be. That focus leads to a plan with action steps. Small daily actions and beliefs lead to magnificent changes.

There is no doubt we will feel pain in life, and we must deal with that pain in a healthy way. We can't pretend it's not there or try to make it go away quickly. There are no shortcuts—reaching the greatest blessing takes hard work.

In John 10:10, remember, Jesus says, "I came that [you] may have life and have it abundantly" (ESV). This is truth. You may have planted a bad seed and reaped a poor harvest in the past, but it's time to plant a new seed, new life, and grow new opportunity. Pivot moments occur when we win the battle in our minds!

You can't change the past, but you can start the process of changing your outlook and yourself. Embrace the moment, seize the opportunity, and move into the bright future God has planned for you.

ABOUT THE AUTHOR

 **DR. JODY G. RAY** was appointed Senior Pastor of Mt. Bethel in May of 2016. Dr. Ray is a second-career pastor, having worked in the financial services sector before entering into ministry. He has a degree in finance and accounting, a Master of Divinity, and a Doctor of Ministry degree. Having experienced many difficulties in the past, Dr. Ray is passionate about coaching people through difficult seasons of life and helping them embrace their futures. Dr. Ray has been married to his wife, Shelley, for fifteen years. They have two incredible daughters, Jennings and Carson, and an adventurous son, Robert. In his free time, Jody enjoys reading, writing, fly-fishing, hunting, and playing golf.

52607064R00095

Made in the USA
Columbia, SC
05 March 2019